Dead Caribou Bags Hunter

By

Keith Evans

© 2002 by Keith Evans. All rights reserved.

No part of this book may be reproduced, stored in a retrieval system, or transmitted by any means, electronic, mechanical, photocopying, recording, or otherwise, without written permission from the author.

ISBN: 1-4033-8666-8 (Electronic)
ISBN: 1-4033-8667-6 (Softcover)
ISBN: 1-4033-8668-4 (Hardcover)

Library of Congress Control Number: 2002095272

This book is printed on acid free paper.

Printed in the United States of America
Bloomington, IN

1stBooks – rev. 11/04/02

DEDICATION

This book is dedicated to my family: my wife, Gail, son Shane, his wife Deborah, granddaughters Stacy and Autumn, daughter Tamlynn, her husband Tom, granddaughters Sayre, Eryl and Ellis, and son Scott, for their support and understanding during my nine years working in Alaska. A special thanks goes to son Scott who came to Alaska to hunt and fish with me on many of the outings.

TABLE OF CONTENTS

1. DEAD CARIBOU'S REVENGE 1
2. HUNTING FOR EELS OR FISHING FOR EELS, WHICH IS IT? 11
3. GILL NETTING THROUGH THE ICE 15
4. NOME THE IDITAROD FINISH 19
5. CARIBOU AND BLACK BEAR AT TAYLOR MT. 24
6. NEW STUYAHOK, ALASKA HUNT 32
7. HUNTING BEAR-BARE 35
8. FIVE GRIZZLIES IN HALF A DAY 54
9. THE BLUEBERRY DEATH MARCH 60
10. CARIBOU HUNT DILLINGHAM, ALASKA 79
11. THE INVASION FROM HAWAII 88
12. WEEKEND CARIBOU 98
13. SUCCESS BREEDS SUCCESS THE RETURN OF THE HAWAII GANG, PLUS 101
14. LET'S DO IT AGAIN! ANOTHER WEEKEND CARIBOU HUNT 113
15. RETIRED, TIME TO HUNT 119
16. BUSH PILOT BLUNDERS 131
17. SOLITUDE AND SURPRISES 141

DEAD CARIBOU'S REVENGE
SEPT. 8, 1997

It's beyond belief that a dead caribou could bag a hunter. That's right, a dead caribou. No, it was not food poisoning. Bang! It got the hunter. No, not the hunter who shot the caribou, but the one who carried its' antlers down off the mountain.

After completing a successful weeks hunt on a remote lake in southwest Alaska where Bob Mills, his two sons, Mike and Joe, Clint Ball, Mike Rosa, my son Scott and I, we returned to my cabin on Lake Aleknagik, Alaska. Bob and his sons then left on a plane from Dillingham, heading back home with their caribou. Bob and Joe were going back to Michigan and Mike was returning to his home in Anchorage. Clint, Mike, Scott, and I were then planning to hunt for a week out of my cabin. We hoped to find moose, caribou, and a grizzly bear.

It was a wet morning as we left the cabin. Mark Vingoe, my partner in the cabin, decided he would rather stay in out of the rain and sleep in, so we left him there. We jumped in my boat and headed down the lake east of the cabin, toward the lower part of Jackknife Mountain. We traveled a couple of miles to an open part on the tundra where Mark shot a moose the year before. We hunted that lower area until about 11:45 a.m. without any luck. We met back at the boat to decide what to do next.

Keith Evans

Figure 1 Jacknife Mountain

"Did you guys see that bull caribou lying down up there on the mountain." I asked.

"Yes", they said they had seen it.

I asked if they wanted to go get it and they were all for it. We headed up the alder covered side of the mountain. After climbing through the alders, tall grass and brush for about an hour, we had second thoughts about our decision. The continued rain didn't make it any nicer.

It was about 2:00 when we came out in the opening near the top of the mountain. Scott and Mike headed east toward where we had seen the bull. Clint and I went northwest up the mountain farther, with a good view of the area where Scott and Mike were headed. We had not gone over a couple hundred yards uphill when we spotted the bull caribou. He was angling toward us away from Scott and Mike. We whistled and got Scott's attention. Our hand signals didn't make much sense to him, but when we started to run northward, he and Mike got the "message" that we saw something. In just a couple minutes we heard several shots, from two different rifles. Clint and I circled the top of the hill we were on, and then headed toward Scott and Mike.

When we saw them they were standing over the bull, which was of modest size. Mike and I set to work dressing it out. Both of them had hit it, but Mike was tagging it. Scott and Clint started glassing the area across the north side of the mountain. Down in the lower part of the drainage they spotted 9 bulls that were feeding, running in circles and feeding again. They also had two other bulls spotted, one of which was a trophy size animal.

Mike and I made short work of dressing out the animal. Within a half hour we had it quartered, the tenderloins, neck, and rib meat removed.

Figure 2 The bull Mike and Scott shot

We sat for a few minutes watching the nine run around and then disappear into the woods on the lower end of the drainage. Scott and Clint decided to try and cut off the trophy bull and his companion that were headed in the same direction the nine had gone. They were not as swift as the bulls and didn't get close enough to shoot. Back they came. We thanked them for the entertainment and chided them for being too slow. Maybe it was a good thing, as packing out another animal for the distance we had to, would not be fun.

It was now 5:00 pm and we were ready to head down the mountain. Scott and Mike each had a hindquarter and front quarter in their pack. Clint had the remainder of the meat in his pack and I had the daypacks and the antlers on my shoulders. Of course we each carried our own rifles. I was not at all enthusiastic about carrying the antlers through neither the thick alders nor the tall grass, which prohibited us from seeing the ground on which we were stepping. The going was difficult and wet. I led the way, trying to find the best way through the alders and brush. At times there was no alternative, but to go directly through thick alders and tall grass. More than once, Clint had to unhook the antlers from alder limbs so I could get through. Sometimes I dragged the antlers and other times they were on my shoulders. There was no good way to carry them. However, it was a hazard for the guys packing out the heavy meat load they had on their backs. The most treacherous areas were those where the grass was so high you could not see the ground on steep downhill slopes. You didn't know if a hole was awaiting your foot or if not a hole, then maybe a stone or uneven surface. It is a wonder someone didn't break a leg. We did go slowly out of common sense and necessity.

At about 6:30 pm we finally got off the mountain and were onto the tundra and lower woods area. We were wet through and through both from the rain and sweating. What a big relief to get out of the alders, brush, tall grass, and off the steep of the mountain. We walked around the edge of a small park and up a hill in a semi –wooded open area. Scott and I had hunted this area earlier in the morning. I decided it was time to take a rest. Scott, Clint and Mike were a little ways behind me with the heavy meat packs. I took hold of my 375 mag with my right hand just below the front sight and set the butt of the rifle on the tundra in front of my right leg. I took hold of the antlers resting on my left shoulder with my left hand and started lifting them off. One of the tines caught in my left pants leg so I twisted to the left to see what the problem was and the next thing I knew I heard a bang and I was lying on my back. My right arm hurt like hell. I grabbed it with my left hand and I felt the bones move. The first thing that went through my mind was that the arm was broken and I had blown an artery. I yelled at Scott, saying, "I need a tourniquet." Scott was about 30 yards behind me and he dropped his pack, as did Clint and Mike who were behind him and they came running toward me. My next thought was, "am I going to die here?"

The three came running up to me and Scott took off his new browning shirt and told. Clint to cut it up into strips. He told Mike to go to the boat, which was about a mile away and go find Mark at the cabin. Mark has a radio in his boat and could use it to get some help.

Mike took off, Clint started cutting and Scott got on his knees beside me and took hold of my arm, around the wound, just below my shoulder. He thought someone had shot me. He said when he heard the gun go off he looked at me and saw things flying off my shoulder. Scott was very cool under pressure. I was very proud of him.

He started wrapping the cut up shirt around my wound, not knowing if an artery was hit or not. It was hard to tell if all the wetness was blood or water from rain and sweat. Scott kept asking me questions as he bandaged me. He had been hit on his bike in Kauai, a few weeks earlier and was lucky to be alive. He knew what questions to ask because the EMT's asked him the questions as he lay on the side of the road after bouncing off a windshield of a car who passed him on a yellow line, as Scott was making a left turn.

Are you dizzy? Do you feel nauseous? Can you see clearly? After several rounds of those questions and others I don't remember, I finally said, "If my eyes are open you can be certain I am alright, so, stop asking me all those questions." I laughed and then told him to stop holding my arm so tight. It hurt like hell. He continued wrapping me with his shirt pieces and I continued to cuss myself for allowing such a thing to happen.

We heard Mike get my motor started just before Scott finished bandaging me. We hoped he would be able to find Mark at the cabin. When Scott put the last piece of bandage on me, I told him to sit me up. He was not very willing to do that. I assured him I was not dizzy, nauseated or insane. He sat me up and I then told him to help me stand. He was even less enthused about doing that. However, like a good son he followed his dads' orders and helped me up. I had decided that I had not hit an artery and that I would much rather be in control of my movements getting back to the shore, than expect others to haul me out by whatever means. I knew my arm would probably hurt the same whether sitting and waiting or walking out. Scott took hold of my left arm and Clint led the way. Besides, my legs were fine and walking would keep me warm and would distract me from thinking about the pain.

We slowly walked the mile or so to the shore where we had left the boat. It took about 30 minutes and was not that difficult. Once we got there, I sat down and put my raincoat back on so I would stay as warm as possible. I was wet from blood, sweat and rain.

Fortunately I had not hit the artery or the nerve, as I could move my arm and fingers. A fraction of an each and I may not have been sitting on the shore waiting for help, but instead, lying on the beach with a tag on my toe.

Figure 3 Lake Aleknagik and peninsula property

We sat on the beach for about 40 minutes before Mike came back. He had found Mark before reaching the cabin and told him what happened, and then continued back to the cabin to get some towels and Scott's backpack. Mark took off down the lake toward the village. Mike got out of the boat with the towels, which were wrapped, around me. They also wrapped a tarp around me, as I was getting cold. More comfort was added by putting me on one of the seats I had in the boat. Scott and Clint had gathered some wood. Of course it was very wet from all the rain, but some gas and oil from cans I had in the boat made for an immediate fire. The only thing missing were marshmallows and hot dogs.

The accident had occurred at 6:38 pm. For some reason, one of the first things I did when I hit the ground was to look at my watch, thinking someone would ask me what time did the accident happen.

We were enjoying the fire for about 30 minutes before two boats and a floatplane arrived. In the plane were Mark and the owner-pilot. It seems that as Mark headed down the lake he contacted the Aleknagik village health center and then called the State Police. He tried to get a helicopter, thinking I was back in the bush someplace, which was logical, because Mike didn't know we had made it to the beach. The helicopter would have to come from King Salmon, at least an hour away. He insisted on one and then after arriving at the beach he found out that a doctor in his floatplane was parked on the beach. He was showing his wife and sister-in-law the area. He was new to Dillingham. Mark asked him for his help and when he agreed, Mark cancelled the helicopter.

Mark got out of the plane and Scott and I got in. We headed for Dillingham and the regional hospital. We had to land on Shannon's Pond just outside Dillingham. Matt Denone was the doctor-pilot and after he landed I kiddingly told him he had better practice his landings, as the two bounces really hurt my arm. He took it very positively.

The ambulance was waiting for us. I walked over and got in and Ron Bowers, along with several other local EMT's took care of me as we headed for the hospital. Once there I was met by a number of friends. My, how quickly the news travels. Doctors Barbara and Richard Asher, Dr. Dave Powers and wife Tawnja, Judy Gonzalves, teacher, Dr. Matt Denone and others whom I forgot, were waiting. I was given some morphine for pain. They cut off my two shirts and dressed the wound. They took off my hip boots and hunting pants, which were kept, but threw away my shorts because they were kind of bloody. Along about 12:00 midnight I was told a medavac team from Anchorage would be arriving to check me out for the trip back to Anchorage. They arrived shortly there after and checked all my vital signs. We departed for Anchorage at about 1:00 am and arrived at the Columbia Regional Hospital in Anchorage at about 2:30 am. Tuesday, Sept. 9, 1997. They took me to the emergency room and gave me some more pain killers

At about 8:30 am 9-9-97, I was on the operating table with Dr. Michael Eaton, orthopedic surgeon. He cleaned out the wound, took some nice pictures, saved the largest chunk of humerus, which he later tied to the rod he inserted inside the humerus.

Scott had made the trip to Anchorage on the plane with me. He got a room, which was just a bed on the 7th floor of the hospital. He called his mother, my wife Gail, back in Michigan earlier, and she was arriving in Anchorage Wednesday night on the 10th. I had told Scott I was not going to call her for a couple of days until I found out just how serious the arm was hurt. . I had bothered enough people already. Hell, I even screwed up the hunting for Mike, Clint and Scott. However, I called Gail right after he informed me she was coming so as not to catch too much hell for not calling her first.

Clint and Mike went back to where the packs had been dropped and hauled them out. They took the meat into Dillingham to the meat processor there. They also helped Mark close up the cabin and took my truck and boat and left it where I keep it at Dave and Tawnja Powers. They came to Anchorage a couple of days earlier than they had originally planned. I really appreciated them packing my stuff and getting all the meat divided and packaged. It was waiting for me at Alaska Airlines Cargo.

It was great to see them when they came over to the hospital. Gail arrived at about 11:00 pm on the 10th. Good thing she came, as she acted as another nurse whenever I needed help. She stayed in the Alaska House room with Scott.

On Friday, Sept. 12, Dr Eaton, had me on the operating table for 4-4 ½ hours. He cut my arm from the wound down to the elbow on the backside of my arm. He had to drill out the humerus because it was too small to accommodate the rod he was putting inside. In the process of putting the permanent rod inside the humerus, he cracked the humerus just above the elbow. The piece of humerus he saved was tied to the rod with wire ties. Screws on both ends of the rod held it firmly inside the humerus. When I woke from the operation I felt terrible. I couldn't see straight. I hurt and felt completely out of control. The remainder of Friday, Saturday and Sunday are pretty much a blur. On Monday, Sept. 15, 1997, Dr Michael Manual, a plastic surgeon, had me on the operating table for two hours. He first took latisimus muscle from my back behind my right arm and placed it in the wound cavity. He then took a thin layer of skin from my right thigh and stapled – stitched it to the piece of skin, which was attached to the muscle from my back and the adjacent skin around the wound opening. A drain was attached to my arm beside the muscle graft and one was placed in my back where the muscle was removed. The drain in my back was taken out before I left Alaska. The one on my arm, after I got to Michigan.

Dead Caribou Bags Hunter

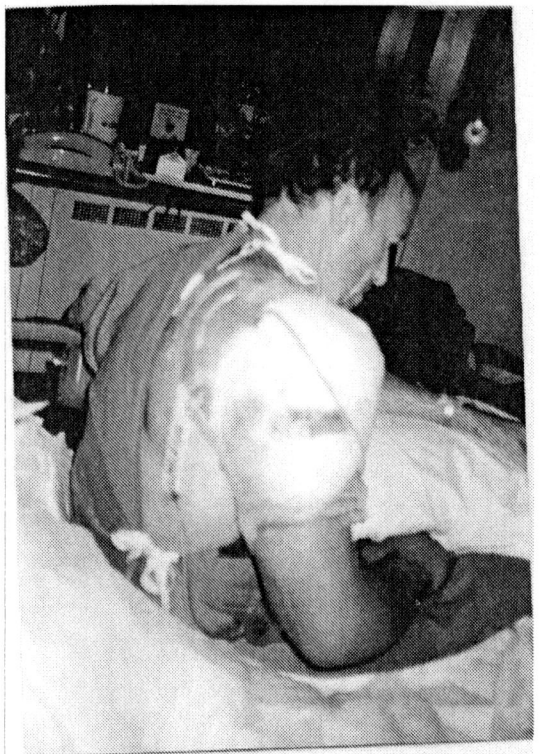

Figure 4 Me after both operations

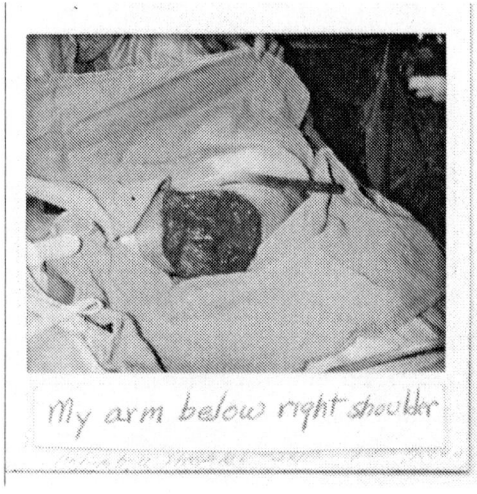

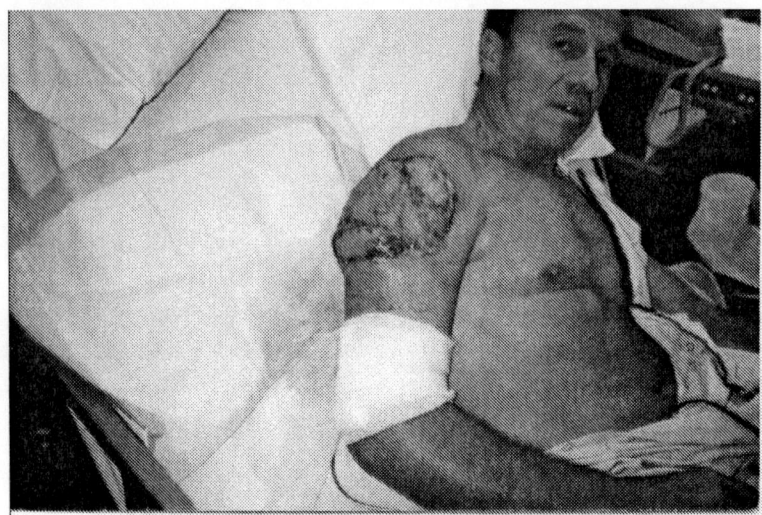
Figure 5 Patch of hide from my leg and back

I was in-patient for 14 days, from 9-9 to 9-23-97. I then went up to Gail's room from 9-23 to 9-29, when we left. During the last week we went to Dr. Manuel's office two days to change dressings and to Providence Hospital three days to have the wound checked.

I was fortunate to be alive.

In May of 2000 I was working in my yard and heard some squeaking coming from my shoulder, as I dug dandelions. I knew WD 40 would not stop it. I got an x-ray and found the noise was coming from the rod that had broke at the second screw from the top of the rod. The rod had fatigued, because the bone had not grown in as expected around the chip, which had been tied to the rod.

In November, instead of whitetail deer hunting on opening day, I was in Rochester, Minnesota's Mayo Clinic getting the rod removed. After taking the rod out, they pulled the humerus together, took bone from my hip and grafted it around the joint and then put a metal plate on the outside of the humerus with twelve screws.

After spending another day in the hospital, I was on my way back to Michigan feeling like a bionic man. The arm is working fine and the last x-rays showed good bone growth.

I hope not to hear any more squeeking.

HUNTING FOR EELS OR FISHING FOR EELS, WHICH IS IT?

OCTOBER 29, 1988

When I was just a kid growing up in northern Michigan we used to fish a lot and as a result would come in contact with fish that had scars from eels. We would look for eels in streams and would try to catch them and kill them. The conservation department of Michigan would also treat streams in an attempt to rid them of spawning eels. As a result, I thought of eels in just one way, they were BAD.

When I went to Alaska to work for the Lower Yukon School District, I lived in a place called Mt. Village. The village of approximately eight hundred Yupik Eskimos is located on the Yukon River. Whenever you live in a different culture one must expect to experience differences in how people live. Have you ever heard of eeling?

Last night after work my neighbor and his wife ask me if I wanted to ride down the "beach" along the Yukon River and see the Eskimos eeling. I said, "yes" and we were off. After driving several miles along the almost frozen Yukon River, over rock, driftwood and sometimes ice, we came to a group of Eskimos standing on the ice. They were waving sticks back and forth with one end of the sticks under the water. As we got closer, I could see eels being tossed out of the water onto the ice. The eels appeared to be temporarily attached to the edge of the stick as it came out of the water and then they would fall off.

There were about eight "eelers" working eeling holes on the ice. Here's how it works. A channel is cut in the ice about a foot wide and eight to twelve feet long, or if some open water can be found that has ice thick enough to stand on along the edge, it will be used. A stick about the size of 2" x 1" and about 10' long is prepared as the "pole" by pounding small nails into the lower outside edges of the stick for about the first 3-4 feet. The nails are pounded in about half way; about a quarter inch apart and then the heads are cut off, which leaves a sharp end. When the stick is swished back and forth under the water the eels that are swimming past are "caught" on the sharp edges of the nails just enough to toss them out of the water onto the ice, where they freeze in short order.

After getting out of the truck we walked over to the fire where several of the children and adults had gathered to get warm. They were making a day and evening of catching eels. We found out that several families would get together to go "eeling" every year. Since the eels come up the Yukon for only a short time each year, the families who catch eels had to know the approximate time to go eeling.

Figure 6 Jean Luc and Yupik man eeling.

We were invited to try our hand at eeling. I took one of the sticks and walked to the edge of the channel cut in the ice. I have to admit I was a little concerned about the thickness of the ice and the current that ran below it. I could see myself breaking through and being pulled under the ice by the current, with no possibility of getting out. So, my approach to the channel was cautious and I chose the one where the biggest man had been standing. My friend, Jean Luc, picked up another "pole" and began eeling. After the first couple of swishes we were flipping eels onto the ice and found the action to be fun.

Judy, Jean Lucs' wife took pictures of us and the eels for the record.

Dead Caribou Bags Hunter

Figure 7 Eel we caught

We talked to the men, their wives and the children about what they did with the eels and they all said they "eat" them and sometimes feed them to their dogs. When they finish eeling for the day, they will divide their "catch" of eels up, without concern about who caught how many.

When looking at the piles of frozen eels on the ice, they reminded me of snakes of the worst kind because of their suction – cup mouth. They were about a foot to a foot and a half long.

Figure 8 Me eeling with a Yupik family.

After accepting about 10 eels to take with us, we 'thanked" them for sharing their "poles' and eeling skills with us and headed back up the beach to Mt. Village. I assumed we took the eels because we wanted to be polite and show them we respected their activity and choice of "food".

As we drove up the beach my neighbors invited me to come over to their house for an eel snack. I could hardly wait. Yum, Yum. I could see that suction-cup mouth looking up at me and their snake like body twisting back and forth. You bet, I was really hungry and anxious to get them on my plate. Should I refuse to broaden my experiences, not be polite to my neighbors and go back on my commitment to learn as much as I could about other cultures while in Alaska?'

What time do you want be to come over?"

"About five," said Judy.

When I arrived at their house I was curious as to how Judy and John Luc fixed the eels. This is what they told me. "You wash them, put them on the broiling pan and cook them until they are crispy—dark brown." Now you may be thinking that they forgot something—no they don't clean them or cut off their head. You cook them whole. The eels were removed from the oven and placed on the table and we sat down to dive into those inviting creatures. The first thing you do is pull off their head and take out their backbone, close your eyes, and nibble! After the first bite I was amazed at how good they tasted, as compared to how they looked. They tasted better than smelt or sardines. This was another case where looks were deceiving. We finished off the platter of eels in short order. So, the next time you go to one of your fancy restaurants, order eel and thank me.

GILL NETTING THROUGH THE ICE
MT. VILLAGE, ALASKA
NOVEMBER 19, 1988

Ya sure, how can you possibly set a gill net under the ice, you ask. Well, I didn't think it was possible when I arrived at this remote village, but the native Yupik Eskimos do a number of interesting things to subsist in this remote area. They manage to have fresh fish for much of the year, even though they also have fish they dry, smoke, can and freeze. While the number of fish they catch during the winter is far fewer than what they catch during the spring-summer-fall, they still have fresh fish when they want it.

How do they manage to get their gill net under the ice? They first find pieces of wood at least 2-3 inches thick and as long as they can find it, but hopefully 8-10 feet long. They then put the ends together, overlapping several feet and tie them together with strong string. They now have a stick from 15 to 20 feet long. On one end of the stick they tie a stout string with a hook or snap on it. They sometimes also tie a piece of wood on the string to make it float. They then spud two holes in the ice a little shorter than the stick. The edges of the ice are beveled so the stick can be shoved into the water up current toward the other hole. While one Eskimo shoves the stick toward the other hole another one waits with a shovel stuck down the hole to catch the string attached to the end of the stick. Once he catches the string he pulls it out of the hole. He then attaches a rope to the end of the string. Once that is done the person holding the end of the stick at the other hole pulls the stick back out of the hole, along with the string and rope attached to the end of it. Next, they untie the rope from the string. The rope is now suspended between the two holes under the ice. They then tie the rope to the end of the gill net. The person at the far hole pulls the rope and the other guides the gill net into the hole and under the ice. If they want to string a long 30-40 foot net they simply cut more holes and do the above. Once the net is under the ice they secure each end by ramming a tree limb at an angle under the ice and secure it there with packed snow and ice. The rope is tied to the limbs on each end. They then use a longer tree limb, about 8' long, to tie to the lower end of the net. When they push the stick down into the water it stretches the net downward. The upper part of the limb is then secured to the other pole now frozen in the ice.

Figure 9 Threading the pole under the ice.

After a day or so they will check their net to see what they have caught. I was fortunate enough to have several friends show me how to put the nets in and then check them Ray and Gary Alexie and Henry Oyoumick took me fishing and showed me how to catch fish using the above method. When we went down to check the net to see if we caught anything, the first thing you had to do was break the ice in the holes and remove it. You then pull up the limb that you used to stretch the net and untie it from the other stick, at both ends. The upper end of the net is untied at one hole and a rope attached. When that is done, the person at the other hole unties the upper rope and pulls the net onto the ice to check for fish. Once fish are removed the person at the other hole will pull his rope and the net will again be pulled back under the ice and secured as before.

Dead Caribou Bags Hunter

Figure 10 Henry and Ray checking net.

Figure 11 Ray and Henry taking fish out of the net.

    I helped with the above operation and today we caught three whitefish. We moved the net to a different spot because that place didn't seem productive enough. We also watched another Eskimo man and his sons fishing in the same way. All rode snowmobiles. While we were setting the nets an Eskimo came by running his dog team and yelled "hello" to us. There is quite a difference between the dogs pulling the sled and the iron horse we had ours attached to.

Figure 12 Mt Village dog team.

Dead Caribou Bags Hunter

NOME THE IDITAROD FINISH
MARCH 15, 1989

What is there to do in mid March if you are in Mt. Village, Alaska? I was standing in my kitchen at around 6:00 p.m. making myself a salad, when I heard a knock on my door. When I opened it, my neighbor Jean Luc was standing there. I asked him to come in and he asked me if I wanted to go to Nome tonight. I asked him for what.

"For the finish of the Iditarod Sled Dog Race," said Jean Luc. He explained that three mushers had already crossed the finish line, but there were others on their way.

Jean Luc said there were six of them going to fly up and I was welcome to go along. They planned on staying overnight and being back home tomorrow by 9:00 a.m. or so. They were going to leave about 7:30 p.m. and expected to arrive in Nome about 9:30. I told him I would think about it.

"How much time do I have?"
"Fifteen minutes," he replied.

Well, I ate my salad and wondered if it would be foolish to spend $100 for the round trip and sleep outside in my sleeping bag in below zero weather. Something inside my head (with horns) said, "go, it is part of the Alaskan experience." After all, I might never get to Nome during an Iditarod Race. I didn't wait for the other voice to speak before I picked up the phone and called Jean Luc to tell him I would go.

What to wear for a fast, cool, overnight trip? On go my long johns, heavy wool socks, turtleneck, wool shirt, insulated pants, insulated vest, flight pants, down jacket and new rabbit hat (town hat). My duffle was filled with my foam pad, sleeping bag, wool stocking hat, some cookies and candy. My camera was made ready with a fresh roll of film. I was ready to go.

I took myself and bag next door and put the bag in Jean Lucs' vehicle. He and his wife, Judy, were ready after a few minutes of friendly bantering. We then headed for the airport. We arrived there at 7:30 p.m. and at 7:45 our plane landed. Inside the plane were

Wayne, pilot, his wife Linda, Larry, a fellow whom I didn't know, and Paul, a fellow who worked at the airport at St. Marys, whom I had seen before. We put out gear in the storage compartment and got into the plane and were ready to –whooooops—leave???? An unexpected serious problem arose. The plane just became a tail-dragger, with nose wheel off the ground. After playing "checkers" with bodies, we finally got the lightest persons seated in the rear and the nose wheel took its correct position on the ground. Now we were ready to leave.

It was a clear and beautiful evening. The sun had disappeared below the horizon. The sky was a golden color, as was the snow line immediately below the horizon. It was a field of gold! Isn't that what Nome is famous for, gold, besides the finish of the Iditarod. We flew across the Yukon Delta toward the Bering Sea and Nome. It was approaching 9:00 p.m. when we reached the Bering Sea and it was almost dark. As we crossed Norton Sound, we looked down to see ice flows that looked like a huge flagstone field. White ice chunks of varying sizes, being "hugged" by clear ice that looked like smooth open water. We wondered if it would hold a plane if an emergency landing were necessary. We could see the lights of Nome just below the horizon, in the far distance. "Another 25 minutes," came the word from Wayne. We buzzed the city on our way to the airport and could see that there was lots of activity going on in the streets of Nome.

After a smooth landing we taxied toward the terminal building and the tie down area. The place where we parked the plane had a plug for the engine heater and would cost $25 for parking overnight. We called a taxi for the mile trip to town. Within five minutes we were getting out of the taxi on Main Street, next to the finish line and the Bering Sea Saloon. The taxi ride cost $21, which Larry took care of for the group. The finish line had bright lights, banners, news reporters, with video cameras, etc. There were lots of people wandering around, mostly in and out of the saloons. We didn't see any mushers around. We were told that one should be along at any time. The fourth place finisher, Dee Dee Jonrowe, was expected soon. Well, rather than stand around in the cold, we decided to step into the Bering Sea Saloon, which was just across the street from the finish line.

It was now getting close to 11:00 p.m. Apparently Dee Dee was having trouble getting her dogs to go. It was said that her dogs had stopped about five miles outside of town at 2:00 pm. in the afternoon and refused to go. It was warm inside the saloon so we didn't mind the waiting. It was unusual that of the seven people in our group, four drank non-alcoholic drinks. (Wayne, Larry, Judy and me. Judy sipped Jean Lucs' and chased it with her coke.)

The Bering Sea Saloon was a long narrow room, with a bar on one side, and a lot of tables and chairs jammed together to get as many people in as possible. On the far side of the room was a stage and a postage stamp size dance floor. We found a table in the crowded room and ordered our drinks. There were all kinds of folks in the saloon. Young, old, natives, whites, singles, couples, groups of women, groups of men, drunks, half drunks, going to be drunks, non-drinkers, a man in shorts, and one in a costume—Spuds. He went around grabbing women and acting like a dog in-heat. I'm not sure how he made out. I do know, he wasn't advertising beer.

A woman came onto the stage and began to play and sing, mostly rock and roll. (Loudly) I heard Judy talking with the two native ladies sitting at the table next to ours. I heard one of them say that she really liked to dance. The next thing I knew she grabbed my arm and asked me if I would like to dance. Well now, I like to dance, but I was in my boots, insulated underwear, insulated pants, turtleneck shirt, and a wool shirt over that. Was I ready to rock and roll? She looked safe enough. She was a typically built native lady with a big smile and lots of pep. Naturally, there was no one else dancing. What the heck, I thought I could do as well as the last guy who was up there on the floor, since he was half drunk. How would anyone know if my stumbling was caused by my boots or too much (pop) to drink. Well, it didn't take long for me to get warm. After two dances I decided it was time to go outside and see if anyone was about to cross the finish line.

Something was stirring down the street. A police car with flashers on was coming towards us slowly and we heard clapping and hollering. Someone was coming. It was Dee Dee. She came running across the finish line ahead of her dog team. She looked exhausted, as did her dogs. After over 1000 miles and 11 days, they had every right to be. After many pictures and an interview, things quieted down for the night, on the streets.

Figure 13 Dee Dee and her team.

Figure 14 The finish line.

    We stood there looking at each other wondering what to do next. The other six said we should go over to the oldest bar in Alaska, the Polaris. Into the Polaris we went. It was another big room, but nothing unique. The dance floor was bigger. The band was a three piecer instead of two. There were younger people and there was a pool table on one corner of the dance floor. Well, we had some unexpected entertainment from the pool players and dancers. After watching the pool players accidentally goose the dancers and drunks bumping into each other and spilling their drinks, I decided I was ready for some sleep. It was now about 2:30 a.m. and the smoke was getting to me. So I told Jean Luc and Judy that I was ready to leave. They agreed. We left the other four to close the bars, eat breakfast, and meet us at the plane at 7:30 a.m.

We decided to walk the mile or so back to the airport. It was about −15 degrees out, but very refreshing. When we got back to the plane we pulled out our sleeping bags and ground pads and layed them on the ground beside the plane and crawled in for a short nap. It was a bit cool. Judy got up during the early morning and changed bags with Jean Luc, but she was still cold. After awhile, she got up and went over to flight service to get warmed up. Jean Luc tried to lure Judy into his bag, but she decided she wanted to get warm, not teased.

At 7:00 a.m. we rolled out and went over to the flight service building to find our four friends lying on the floor; two sleeping and two drinking coffee. After sharing my cookies and lies about our comfortable night in our sleeping bags, we got in the plane and took off.

It was 7:45 a.m. and we witnessed a beautiful Alaska sunrise, which was soothing to our sleepy eyes. I was back at work by 9:30 a.m.; glad I took advantage of another Alaskan opportunity.

Keith Evans

CARIBOU AND BLACK BEAR AT TAYLOR MT. AUGUST—1990

I was employed by the Lower Yukon School District as superintendent and Dale Lackner was a teacher in the village of Marshall, Alaska. Dale is a pilot and owns his own plane. We had talked several times in the past when I visited Marshall, about hunting, both in Alaska and our respective home states of: Montana and Michigan. Dale had been a hunting guide in Montana before coming to Alaska to teach. He had been in Alaska several years prior to my arrival in 1988. As a result, he had used his plane to get him to various good hunting spots in Alaska. One place where he had gone several times was Taylor Mountain. In a recent conversation he mentioned he had a friend who was bringing his son to hunt in early August for caribou. They were coming from Wyoming. Dale invited me to accompany them to Taylor Mountain. I accepted.

Since I had a long time friend, Tom Sheets, who lived in McGrath, which is on the way to Taylor Mountain, I decided to take Tom up on an earlier invitation to fish salmon with him sometime. Since salmon would be running up the river to spawn the first of August, I could go fishing first and then go hunting, all on the same trip. Tom had taught in McGrath for a number of years before retiring and becoming the owner of a Bed and Breakfast business there.

I flew to McGrath August 6, 1990. Tom met me at the airport. We spent the evening exchanging memories of the past years in high school. Tom grew up in Boyne City, Michigan and I grew up in East Jordan, ten miles away. Our schools played in the same athletic conference and we were both athletes in all the sports. Needless to say we had fun differing on who had the best teams and athletes over the years. Tom had come to Alaska early in his teaching career and then returned to Michigan for a year, during which time he taught science in my building at Traverse City Jr. High. I was the building principal for about 800 ninth graders. Tom and I would meet each morning early enough to run the hills across from the school, shower and be ready for students when they arrived.

Dead Caribou Bags Hunter

The next morning after my arrival, we jumped in Tom's boat, along with a friend of his and headed up the Kuskowhim River. After traveling over 120 miles of river and several stops to fish for pike in the sloughs, we arrived at a remote cabin on the Salmon River, a tributary. We were anxious to fish for salmon, so we grabbed our rods and started casting before unloading the boat. Tom caught five salmon on his first five casts, his friend got seven for seven and I caught three on my first three casts. We caught and released most of the salmon until our arms were tired. We then unloaded the boat and had something to eat.

We spent the night at the cabin, fished several hours the next morning with the same results and then departed back to McGrath. Of course we had to stop and catch some more large pike in several sloughs before getting there. It was great fishing. Tom mentioned after we had seen about the tenth moose, that he annually would get a moose while hunting along the river. The largest moose he got during his 14 years in McGrath had an antler spread of 73 inches. That is big.

Tom took me to the airport the next morning to meet Dale, Val and son Justin. We loaded my gear into Dale's plane and headed to Taylor Mountain, about 120 air miles away. It was a beautiful sunny day and the scenery over the rivers was awesome. We were headed for an abandon mine where there was a good gravel runway. As we approached it we could see two tents adjacent to it. Apparently there were some other hunters ahead of us. We landed and tied down the plane after pushing it off the runway.

After getting our tents set up and gear put away, we fixed something to eat. Dale shared some stories of two previous successful hunts here at Taylor Mountain. On one of the hunts he brought two native friends who got three caribou after shooting 15 times. More caribou could have been taken, but they would have exceeded the maximum load the plane could carry safely. The other hunting trip almost ended in disaster. Dale and friend had loaded their gear, meat and antlers into the plane in a hurry to leave before the whiteout they could see coming, reached them. They took the wing covers off, put them in the plane, started it and then could not see a thing. It was snowing, with freezing rain and fog. They quickly decided to put the wing covers back on to prevent ice buildup and took their tent our and set it back up. The next morning they woke up to about a foot of snow, on top of what had already been on the ground. It was very foggy out. How were they ever going to get out, as it was October 31 and the winter was just starting? They decided that the plane could not take off going down a deep snow covered runway. From morning until late evening they tramped snow for the wheels to follow down the runway. They had not finished tramping the full length, but the fog lifted and they rushed to leave. Off came the wing covers and down came their tent. They started the plane and let it warm up to the minimum and started down the runway. As they got to the end of the tramped area they were still not airborne, but Dale had planned ahead. He had his buddy handling the flaps. The plane had enough speed to continue though the initial unstamped snow, but started to slow, Dale told his buddy to pull the flaps a notch. They lifted off, and then dropped down again to hit the snow on the runway. They bounced up and barely stayed above the ground high enough to miss the trees at the end of the runway. All had a very scary experience!

We were not worrying about snow because it was very warm. In fact, so warm I was concerned about the meat being Ok if we got any caribou in the next two days.

Dale mentioned that there were lots of black bear around and we should also be looking for them, in addition to our prime target, caribou. We decided to all leave camp together and head up the drainage behind the tent. We had just got nicely started when this years calf caribou stepped out of the alder bushes in front of us about 50 yards away. I got out my video camera and started recording. She probably had never seen a human before, as she stood looking at us and then walked several steps, smelling us. She had a pretty white nose and ears. After stopping she looked at us for a moment or two, then turned around and trotted up the drainage and back into the alders.

Val and Justin left Dale and me to hike along the vary top of the small mountain we were climbing. Dale and I traversed it below the very top and encountered a cow caribou trotting parallel to our path. She stopped and gave us the eye, before continuing across the open tundra. We went over several small ridges and finally stopped to glass across a valley in a fork of the drainage we were following.

There were some alders on the hillside opposite of us and just above the alders we could see a large bull caribou. He was feeding on lichen. Dale gave me a rundown on the length of his antlers, with the closing remarks, "he is a real trophy." We watched him feed for about half an hour before he went into the alders. Dale thought the flies were bothering him as he shook his head a number of times just before going in.

We spotted Val and Justin walking the very ridge of the mountain, sky lined. After waving at them for about ten minutes, they finally understood our "message," to come over to us. When they arrived, we told them about the bull caribou and our plan to get him. The plan was for them to circle up the hill and get above the alders where he was and we would head across the side of the hill we were on to get closer to the alders. We would still be across the valley, but within a couple hundred yards of the alders. Dale took my video camera to record the coming action. As Val and Justin got across from, but still below the alders, I saw what at first appeared to be two bull caribou coming out of the alders. No, there was just one, but his antlers were so wide apart it tricked me into thinking there were two bulls. He started down the hill towards us. I shot from my knelling position and he turned broadside running parallel to us.

Dale was saying, "Where did you hit him?" "Wait, wait until he stops, now."

I fired just before he said, "now." When my bullet hit him the dust flew and he dropped dead.

We hiked across the valley and up the hill to find a real nice trophy bull caribou. He was still in velvet, with a double shovel and very long main beams. After taking pictures, we dressed him out, cut up the meat and packed him the half-mile to camp. Because the weather was so warm I decided to put the meat in plastic bags and submerge them in the creek near the runway.

As we were eating breakfast the next morning our neighbors flew out. We didn't see them with any antlers, so we don't know how they did hunting. It was just a bit before 5:00 am when we got up, as it gets light early and stays light late at this time of year. We decided to head out of camp in a different direction this morning. After staying together for about half an hour of walking, I decided to split off and head up a valley. They continued up over a ridge and out of sight.

Keith Evans

About an hour later I heard several shots that were spaced a little while apart. I had just topped a hill at the upper end of the valley and could see across a flat area of open tundra. There, about 150 yards away was a black bear feeding on blueberries. I got down on hands and knees and started crawling towards him. I wanted to get at least 50 yards closer, chancing scaring him since there was no cover for me to hide behind. I had crawled about ten yards when he stood up and looked in my direction. Was I another bear or what? Maybe he thought I was a grizzly bear, because he dropped down on all fours, turned and ran about five bounds then stopped and looked at me. I had my gun to my shoulder hoping he might do just that. Just as I squeezed the trigger he jumped forward, but not far enough to avoid my bullet. He rolled, then righted himself and ran straight away into a low area of alders and tall grass. I stood up and walked to where I saw him disappear. I was not enthused about going into the tall grass and alders. There was no blood or sign to follow and I could not see over ten feet in any direction. However, I would not leave a wounded animal to suffer. I slowly entered the undercover, thinking to myself I was crazy. I searched part of the alders in the acre or so patch, but could not find him. I was not happy about that, but apparently I either did not go far enough or just not to the right spot, if he were down. If he were not down, he could certainly move as he heard me coming.

I left the alders and headed in the directions where I heard the shots. I assumed they may have gotten a caribou and were still there. When I found them, they had just finished skinning a black bear. It seems they had topped a ridge coming out of the alders and looked out across the open tundra and Dale spotted the bear, about 200 yards away. They all bent down and slowly got to within about 150 yards and Justin sat down and took a shot. He missed, so Val shot and hit him in the rear. The bear ran into the alders. Dale went into the alders, while Val and Justin watched. The bear didn't come out nor did Dale see him in the alders. They decided to continue hunting for caribou and had walked to the top of a little knoll, when they spotted the bear. Justin shot and hit the bear in the ribs and it ran into a small patch of alders. Dale and Val walked around the backside of the alders while Justin waited opposite of them. The bear had been bellowing as it entered the alders and for a few minutes while there. Then all was silent. Dale and Val went into the alders and there lay the bear, dead. What they did notice while skinning him was that his front leg had been broken near his foot, which must have been painful.

It was decided that Justin would take the hide back to camp and Dale and Val would continue hunting for caribou. I decided to go back and wait around the alders where my bear had gone to see if he might come back out. He didn't.

Justin was back in camp with his bear hide stretched out and salted, when I arrived early that evening. We ate, after waiting several hours for Val and Dale. We were in our sleeping bags when we heard them coming into camp. I looked at my watch and it read, 11:15 p.m. It was almost dark, as my video will attest. They had walked up another drainage after leaving me and spotted two bull caribou. As they worked their way toward them they noticed several bigger caribou in the far distance beyond the two they were stalking. They circled past the first two bulls they saw and were nearly to the top of the hill they were climbing, when Val told Dale to go on up and check the other bulls. He was going to check the two they had just circled around. When Dale came back down towards him, Val asked Dale to evaluate the bull to see if he was a shooter. Dale looked through his binoculars and told him the bull was too small. They then went over the hill after the bigger bulls. Well, they decided after trying to catch up with the bigger bulls for half an hour of walking, that it just wouldn't happen. Dejected, they turned and headed back to camp. It was getting late evening and it would take them an hour to get back to camp. When they were about a half-mile from camp they spotted the two bulls they had seen earlier. They had walked about a half-mile closer to camp from where they had last seen them.

Dale said, "that one is a nice bull, shoot him."

Val said, "you told me earlier he was too small."

Dale said, "I was looking at the other one."

Val took aim and shot. He missed. The second shot dropped the bull. They were very tired at this point, but were dragging when they got to camp with full packs of meat and the antlers.

Keith Evans

The next morning Dale could hardly walk. He had blisters on his feet from walking from 5:15 am to 11:15 pm. He said he would spend the day in camp processing the meat and bear hide. Part of the morning was also spent scoring my antlers. Dale was experienced at it so he did the measuring. My bull scored 348, which is under the 425 needed for the record book. My bull lacked the long upper tines, which would have put him in the book. His main beams were as follows: left side- 55 inches and right side—52 inches. It had a double shovel, but only one was pal mated. Val's bull was a nice size one, but not as large as mine. Both were in velvet.

Val and Justin went out and were successful in finding a medium size bull for Justin. When they got back to camp we decided to pack up and leave later that day. At about 4:00 pm, August 11, 1990, we took off back to McGrath. On the way we saw four different forest fires, which were apparently started from lightning strikes. They would burn themselves out.

We got back to McGrath, where I got out and said my "thanks and farewells." Tom Sheets came down and helped me haul my meat and antlers to a walk-in cooler that a friend of his had graciously consented for me to use until my flight out later that evening. I wanted to mount the head and keep the velvet on the antlers. Keeping them cool would stop the velvet from slipping. It was about 70 degrees out and leaving them out would certainly prevent that from happening. Several hours later I boarded the plane for Anchorage and I noticed my antlers sitting on the ramp waiting to be put on the plane. When I got to Anchorage, my antlers did not arrive with me. They had left them sitting on the ramp and 24 hours later they arrived. The velvet had started to slip and when I got them to the taxidermist, he had to remove all of it. However, the head mount looks very good on my wall, even though there is no velvet on the antlers.

Dead Caribou Bags Hunter

Figure 15 Me and my bull.

Keith Evans

NEW STUYAHOK, ALASKA HUNT
9-12. 13-92

Mark Vingoe and I went up to New Stuyahok, a small village on the Nushagak River, to go hunting for caribou, moose and bear. We left on Friday night after school and flew the 60 miles from Dillingham. Since Mark worked for Southwest Region Schools, we had access to stay in their maintenance building, which had a bank of beds, a shower, stove, toilet, etc.

We got up the next morning about 7:00 and went over to Ron and Angie Martinez's home for breakfast. At about 10:30 we were finally ready to go up river. We inflated Mark's zodiac and loaded it full of gear. Mark always takes more than needed. I was wondering if there was room to sit down in the boat. For a while I thought we might have to attach a rope to the front and drag it from shore. Food alone cost $180. He even bought two pints of blueberries for $2.79 each, plus other gourmet items.

Rod Mebius, Principal at New Stuyahok, and Jeff, a friend from Oregon, and Ron would be in one boat and Mark and I in Mark's boat. We were headed up to a cabin that the school district students had built years ago as part of their educational program. It was located on a tributary river called the Mulchatna. We would stay there over night and motor up the Mulchatna looking for game.

It was a beautiful morning as we headed up river. We stopped and put our gear in the cabin and then continued up the river hunting. We saw a heard of about 20 caribou running along the riverbank. I was driving our boat with Mark in the bow. He shot one caribou and the other boat shot one also. We dressed them out on the riverbank and loaded them in the boats. We saw a couple of cow moose, but no bulls, nor any bear. We did see some other hunters who had gotten caribou.

As we headed back down the river we stopped whenever we came upon open tundra to glass for caribou. On one stop we glassed across the tundra and Mark saw some caribou antlers, but no body below them. On a closer look, what we found was the skull supporting the horns. Apparently the animal had died by some means. Could have been wolves or possibly a bear. Farther down the river, but on the

Dead Caribou Bags Hunter

same side and in the same open park, Rod, Ron and Jeff could be seen sneaking toward a small herd of caribou. We sat down to watch. There was a small patch of brush the guys were headed for to get close enough to shoot. When they got behind the bushes they were about 100 yards away from the caribou. Bang, down when one bull and the others took off running. Several more shots were fired, but no caribou where hit. After dressing their bull, they had a long pack back to the boat. Fortunately, there were three of them to pack the meat so none had too heavy a load. We all headed down river to New Stuyahok and then Mark and I were on a plane for Dillingham.

On Sept. 19 & 20 I went back up to New Stuyahok again. Ron, Rod, Jeff and I went back out to the cabin. On Saturday afternoon Ron and I drifted down the Mulchatna, after motoring up it several miles without seeing anything. I happened to look back up river behind us and saw six caribou standing on the bank. They must have come out of the woods after we had gone past them. They stood on the bank for just a moment and then went down the bank into the river and started swimming across. I started the engine and headed back up after them. I caught up to them before they were out of the water. Ron was seated in the front of the boat with gun ready. Since you are not allowed to shoot a game animal while in a boat under power, we waited until they were on the bank and I shut the engine off, and then Ron shot several times, but hit nothing. The last bull, the biggest one of the bunch, made a foolish mistake and started running parallel to the river, instead of going into the brush. That gave me time to shoot. One shot and he fell. We pulled the boat in, dressed the caribou and had just a step or two to put the meat in the boat. The easiest pack I have ever had while hunting.

We stayed in the cabin Saturday night and got up and headed back up river the next morning. We saw several bull moose and cows, but couldn't get a shot. We were heading back down river to the cabin and decided to check the slough where we had seen the first bull earlier that morning. We got back to the same spot and there on the opposite bank stood a bull moose looking at us. I was in the bow of the boat and Rod was in the stern. We both shot at exactly the same time and the bull dropped in his tracks on the bank. He was not quite dead so I gave Ron my 44-mag pistol and he got out and shot him behind the ear. The bull had a rack that was about 50" across. With all of us working we had it quartered and in the boat within an hour. We headed back to the cabin, picked up our gear and pulled into New Stuyahok in the early evening. I took the two hindquarters and left the rest of the meat with Rod and Ron.

When I got back I took the meat over to Mark's and hung it in his garage, since the weather was in the high 30's, it aged well.

Figure 16 Me and my moose.

Dead Caribou Bags Hunter

HUNTING BEAR-BARE
MAY 1992

    Mark Vingoe, a fellow school administrator from Dillingham, Alaska was trying to arrange a brown bear hunt on the Alaskan Peninsula for us during the spring season, May 10 – 25. He finally gave up on trying to get us out on the Peninsula. There were no pilots or planes available. He tried to arrange something up one of the rivers in the Dillingham area. One of his school principal friends from one of the remote villages was going to loan him a boat and motor so we could go up river to where the grizzlies could be found. Unfortunately, the spring had been cold and the snow had not melted much so the river was still too low to allow anyone to travel up river. Mark finally gave up on that idea. He had also tried to find a pilot who might fly us into a remote spot and land on a ridge or a sandbar. The only pilot who was interested in doing that was also interested in making some sure money flying for herring fishermen. The fishermen are given rather short notice when there would be an opening, so the pilot was really on hold for them and therefore could not set anything up with us that was definite. Pilots are employed by the fishermen to go spot the schools of herring so the fishermen will know exactly where to go to catch the most fish. On the 20th of May, then days after we had planned on hunting, Mark finally gave up and said we would have to plan a fall hunt down on the Peninsula.

    I decided that I still wanted to go bear hunting someplace. It was getting close to the end of the season by this time, so I called the Fish and Game Department and asked them to recommend a place where I could drive to from Anchorage, and then hike into the wilds for a bear hunt. The Anchorage office referred me to their Tok office. I called them and they gave me directions to Dry Creek, a spot between Delta Junction and Tok. The told me that the caribou were generally having calves on the plateaus about a days hike above Dry Creek. All I needed to do was find the trail and hike up there. According to them there generally was a good concentration of grizzlies that followed the caribou when they were calving.

    Since I knew the superintendent of schools who lived in Tok, he being an avid hunter and familiar with that area, I gave him a call and shared with him what I had been told by Fish and Game. When I told him I was hunting alone, he said, "get up here." So at 3:00 pm, Thursday, May 21, 1992, I jumped in my truck and headed for Tok, 326 miles north of Anchorage. I arrived there at about 10:00 that night. It was a beautiful scenic drive. I saw six moose and three sheep along with some fantastic snow capped mountains, wide river basins, and the Matanuska Glacier.

The superintendent, Spike Jorgensen, his wife Pearl, and sons Ronk and Thor greeted me when I arrived. It was obvious they were a hunting family, since there were many head mounts of sheep and deer on the walls, along with some tanned bear hides and lots of pictures. In the basement I saw many skulls of sheep and bear that they had taken over the years in Alaska. They also had many green hides from wolves and martin taken during trapping season.

After some general conversation and hunting talk we loaded my gear into Spike's super cub for the 6:00 am departure the next morning. I got some shuteye on the couch even though it seemed like I had just blinked before getting up. When I looked out the window I was greeted with some cloudy skies and a bit of rain in the air. Spike and I grabbed a quick bite to eat and then went out to his hanger. We pushed the plane out and jumped in. Spike lives next to the airport and can taxi directly to the runway from his house. Very convenient to say the least. Spike fired it up and taxied to the active runway. It seemed like we had only traveled a few feet and the cub was off the ground. Spike had just gotten the plane and was getting the feel of it so he did a touch and go, then we headed toward the hunting area. Before getting out of town, Spike did another touch and go at the deserted military runway just outside of Tok. We flew out a river basin and over the area the Fish and Game Department had recommended. The area was still snow covered and we could not see a single caribou, nor tracks that they had been there. I was sure glad I did not take the time and effort to hike back into that country to find out the caribou and grizzlies were not there. What to do?

Spike decided to go to a place where he had seen some bear and where he had helped some friends build a cabin. It was a small lake not too far from the area we had just flown over. As we approached the lake I could see the ice had melted away from the shoreline in front of the cabin and the ice was a bit dark colored. I asked Spike if it was safe to land on it and he assured me it had plenty of ice to hold us up. We landed on T Lake. Spike said it would be fine for me to stay in the cabin and to use the boat on the shore. The area was heavily wooded with evergreens so there were not many places where I could glass for bear. Right behind the cabin, which was located up the hill from the lakeshore, there was a semi-open ridge that had some poplar trees on it, which made for a possible viewing area.

After landing on the ice, Spike and I got out and walked around. The ice seemed solid, even though it had melted away from the shoreline in a number of places along the eastern area of the lake. There was about a 20-foot gap of open water in front of the cabin. On the south end of the lake the ice was up against the shore. After talking about what my other options were, we decided that this spot was probably as good as any, especially since there was a cabin to stay in. I unloaded my gear onto the ice, figuring I would walk across the lake to where the ice was up against the bank. That was probably a mile or so. Once off the lake I would walk around the shoreline to the cabin and then take the boat and get my gear off the ice. I felt a little uneasy about the ice, having had scary experience years earlier of falling through the ice and it looked much safer than this ice. This ice was dark colored and looked as if it were ready to break up. I mentioned to Spike that the only concern I had was with the ice. He reassured me that there was plenty of ice and it would be fine. I figured he must know, having lived here for a number of years and the fact he was willing to land his plane on it.

Spike said he would pick me up on Monday at noon and he then jumped in his plane and took off. He circled the lake and when he got over the top of me he pointed back toward the western shoreline. I had already taken my gun and pulled up my hip boots and was headed for the south shore. After he gave me the west signal I knew he meant the ice was by the bank and it was half the distance to walk on the ice. As I headed to the west my eyes were on the ice and the different colors, along with different surface conditions made me rather uneasy. I looked over my shoulder as I walked to the west and Spike was just a speck in the sky, as he headed back to Tok. I was looking at the ice and reminding myself that Spike had said that there was about three feet of ice on the lake. When I was about 200 yards from shore, without warning, my left leg went through the ice up to my hip. I fell forward onto my hand holding the gun, and hitting my right knee. I took the gun in my right hand and hit the butt of it on the ice in front of me as I moved forward on my right knee. I pulled my left leg out of the hole and decided to stand up, as the ice did not crack when I hit it with the butt of my gun. I was scared, not knowing if the next step would mean going through the ice with both feet or one foot. I took several steps forward and I heard the terrible sound of cracking ice. I wanted off the ice immediately. I reminded myself that I should have followed my first instinct and that was not to stay and use the ice for a hunting base. It would do no good to wish now, as I was here and I had a serious problem. I had to get off the ice as soon as possible. I took another step and the ice cracked again. Slowly I turned and slid my feet across the ice back towards the south end of the lake. It was a much longer walk, which would mean many fearful steps. I circled back around the hole in the ice and tensed as I put weight on each foot, sliding them more than walking. As I headed south, I watched the ice for any sign that my next step would be on honeycombed ice. Something felt sticky in my left hand. I looked at it and it was bloody. I apparently cut my hand when I fell forward as my left leg went through the ice. The cut was the least of my concern at that moment. With all the excitement I had not felt the ice cut my hand.

    I knew I wanted off the ice as soon as possible. I kept watching the shoreline for a place to get off the ice before going the full distance to the south end. There was a small peninsula jutting out on the east shoreline and it appeared that the ice came close to the bank. I turned and headed in that direction. Several times I felt for sure that the next step would cause the ice to break. It just appeared to be more rotten looking the closer I got to the shoreline. As I got closer to the shore I could see that the ice did not reach the shore, but had open water for 10-15 feet. I stopped and asked myself did I want to take a chance of swimming that distance or should I walk to the south end. I decided that the water might be shallow that close to shore and I would go for it. As I stepped gingerly toward the open water the ice beneath my feet started to submerge underwater and then it broke. I went through—up to my waist. I was able to push my way through the ice and reach shore safely. What a relief!

Dead Caribou Bags Hunter

I got out on shore and took off my boots and drained the water out and wrung out my pants. The walk around the shoreline to the cabin warmed me up and calmed down my nerves. About and hour and one half later I was beside the boat ready to go get my gear off the ice, or was I? I did not like the thought of going back on the ice, even with the boat.

I got the boat turned over and found several oars under it. I launched the boat and jumped onto the bow. Sitting on the bow, I used the paddle to pull me across the open water to the edge of the ice. I started breaking the ice with the paddle until it got too thick. I then started breaking it with my foot. With one foot in the boat and one foot out breaking ice, I finally got to solid ice that I could not break. I carefully put weight on my left foot, which was on the ice, making certain it would hold me before swinging my right foot out of the boat. Finally, I was able to step out with my right foot, standing erect, but still holding onto the side of the boat. No, I did not walk over and pick up my gear. I pulled the boat along side of me, put my gear in it and retraced my steps. As I approached the edge of the ice on my return trip, I moved to the stern of the boat and pushed it into the water and jumped in. With a few paddles I was to shore and on firm ground. What a relief!

Well, I came to hunt so I thought I would head up to the cabin with my gear and then explore. I put the pack on my back and carried my rifle and other items up the steep slope to the cabin, which was about 100 yards away. It was enough of a climb to get my heart beating, just as if I needed mine to be beating any faster that it already had been today. The first thing that I noticed as I approached the cabin was that one of the windows had been broken and there where claw marks on the siding below it, from a bear. Would I have another surprise? Was the bear still inside or had he not gone in? I carefully opened the door and peered inside with rifle at ready. No bear.

It was a nice Lincoln log cabin with several windows in the front and back. It had several rooms along with a Coleman stove, dishes, pans, etc. I even found some food, which I didn't need. Also there was a deck of cards and an ax. The cards would prove to be helpful in passing some time away. After unloading my gear and repairing the window, I fixed myself something to eat and sat on the ridge in a lawn chair overlooking the lake. It was now about 1:00 pm and the sun was getting very warm.

Hunting was what I came to do so I thought I would take off and do some exploring behind the cabin. I walked for about a half hour and reached a ridge that was fairly open. I sat down and stayed in that spot for the afternoon. I did not see anything except for some birds. I did however, do a lot of thinking. It was mostly about how fast the ice would melt and having to walk back out on it to get in the plane. I was not thrilled with the idea.

Figure 17 Me hunting by the cabin.

I decided that there might be a bear working the shoreline, looking for something to eat so I walked back to the cabin and sat in the chair on the ridge, glassing the shore area for several hours. Nothing. The sun was warm and it was very peaceful, except that I could imagine the ice breaking under my feet as I watched the heat waves shimmering above the lake surface. It must have been at least 70 out today. After some more sitting and glassing, it was now 10:30 pm and I was feeling tired, even though there would be daylight for a total of 19 hours. I decided to unroll my sleeping bag and try out the bunk bed. I got my inflatable mattress out and put it on top of some Styrofoam and put my bag on top of that. I found my little flashlight and put it beside me and then hung my gun up on a small nail, beside the bed. I was now ready for mosquitoes or bear. It didn't take me long to go to sleep even though it was still light outside. As you may know, it really doesn't get very dark in Alaska in the summer time.

I awoke suddenly! What was it that I heard? The first thing that I thought of was a bear. Was one trying to get into the cabin? I listened carefully. I was sleeping in the room where the window had been broken by the bear. Maybe he was trying to get in again. Then I heard a familiar noise. Mosquitoes looking for a place to land and plant their needle noses. I snapped on my flashlight and flicked the beam around until I spotted the two mosquitoes making all the noise and I dispatched them with my shirt and sleeping bag. I finally got back to sleep after thinking about one of those big mosquitoes landing on me and sucking me dry of blood before I could wake up. Wake up I did, at a rather early hour of 4:00 a.m.

After a hurried breakfast I went out to the ridge behind the cabin and spent several hours looking for grizzly bear. Nothing showed up. I went back to the cabin and had some more to eat and decided to execute the plan I had formulated while sitting on the ridge earlier in the morning. I decided that the fewer steps I took on the ice the better. Therefore, walking around the lake to the south end and then walking better than a mile back to where the plane would land was not my idea of fun. I figured the best thing to do was to find a way to get onto the ice as close to where the plane would land as possible. That meant I had to get across open water without swimming or using the boat. A raft was the solution. I figured I could use the boat to pile my gear on the ice, take the boat back and then take my raft out to the ice and walk the short distance to the plane. Good idea! I took the ax that was in the cabin and went down to the edge of the lake where I found lots of old dead trees devoid of limbs. What a nice surprise. I would not have to do any trimming of limbs nor cut down any trees. These old dead poles where made to order. I found some still standing and others already on the ground. I hauled them to the spot where I wanted to launch the raft and began the process of cutting the poles to the proper length. After cutting about 10, I got a rope and tied the poles together in two places. I then found a long pole to push me through the water and launched my raft. I stepped onto the raft and whoops. It was very unstable and started to roll around. That would not do. I decided it would need some poles underneath and perpendicular to the top logs. I went back to shore and found six logs, cut them to the length I wanted, and forced them under the raft. It looked much more stable, so I picked up my pushing pole and mounted the raft. Terrific, I didn't roll or sink. I pushed myself out to the edge of the ice and hit it with my pushing pole. The ice busted. Another problem. How was I going to step onto the ice without it breaking? The only thing I could think of was that I needed to distribute my weight over the ice and the only way I could do that was to make a walkway with some poles. Back to shore. I found three poles each about 20 feet long and took them back out to the ice. I broke the soft ice away and then put the three side by side. I was about to step on them for a test and then thought better of it. It would be wiser to get the boat and have it along side of me, just in case the logs didn't hold me up. Back to shore and over to the boat. Back to my ice walk with the boat. With one foot in the bow of the boat and one on the walkway, I lifted the boat and walked with one foot in the boat and one on the walkway. It would be safe. Terrific. Back to shore with a relieved mind, plus some blisters on my hands and some red skin on my body from the sun. It was warm and I had stripped off my shirt and as a result got rather sunburned.

    I enjoyed the rest of the day. I just sat around and enjoyed the sun and the wildlife of mostly ducks and swans. I did see a bald eagle and some hawks flying around looking for something to eat. The eagle flew over with a fish in his claws. While I sat looking and listening I had my doubts about the ice holding until Monday, even though it froze last night. I decided to check the ice. I took the ax and went down and jumped into the boat. A few minutes later I was breaking the ice trying to find some solid enough to hold the boat and me. After breaking some for about 10 feet I finally hit solid ice and I pulled the boat out of the water and hauled it along beside me as I walked toward the area where Spike would land. I cut into the ice and after chopping about a foot I decided it was OK. I was a bit more optimistic that I would get out Monday, even though the ice had melted another 10 feet away from shore.

    Sunday night was cloudy and it rained a bit so it was too warm to freeze. The ice did not look very good Monday morning. I wished I had told Spike to come early instead of at noon, to take advantage of any freeze, which might have occurred over night. Unfortunately, I told him to come at noon and it did not freeze over night. At about

8:30 a.m. I decided I had better go out on the lake and test the ice again. I found two long poles to take with me just in case the ice was not safe enough for Spike to land. The poles would be placed on the ice in a cross design which means the runway is closed. I jumped in the boat and paddled the ever-widening gap between the shore and the ice. There was now about 40 yards of open water to cross. I sat in the bow of the boat and paddled until I got to the ice. I noticed that the logs I had placed on the ice for my walkway had about three feet of pole in the water because the ice had melted that much in the last twelve hours.

Figure 18 Melting ice away from the shore.

I started breaking ice with one foot while keeping the other in the boat as before. After breaking about 15 feet of ice, I couldn't break any more so I stepped out of the boat with my left leg so as to pull the boat onto the ice, as I had done before. I started to lift the boat, then the ice broke and I went through up to my hip. I pulled the boat over onto my leg in an effort to stop sinking farther. As I did, the boat almost turned over on top of me. It was on top of my leg, which was through the ice. I could see myself with the boat upside down on top of me and more ice breaking away. With a big heave I pushed the bow away from me and off my leg. When that happened the boat turned upright and no longer rested on my leg. Grabbing onto the bow I pulled myself into the boat. At that moment I decided I would not want Spike to land of the lake nor would I walk on it. I took the two poles out of the boat and placed them onto the ice in a cross design, so Spike would not land.

When Spike came a few minutes later, fortunately I was still in the boat, so I signaled him with the oars, making a cross sign so he would know not to try landing. Spike flew around a few minutes and I got out of the boat and walked up in front of the cabin. He flew low and dropped me a note. He gave me several options and the signal to make to him for the option I wanted. There was a signal for an emergency pick-up by helicopter; one for staying three more days; one for staying 5 more days; another for getting a floatplane to pick me up; and one if I needed more food. I was wondering if he could remember all the signals and options as he flew around while I was reading his note. I decided the best option was for the floatplane, which also was his number one recommendation. I waved my jacket as that signal and hoped we communicated. He wagged his wings and headed back to Tok. His note said he would be back Tuesday night. I began to accept staying for several more days, still thinking I would make it out by Thursday so I could keep my dental appointment, which I had waited a month to get. I was however, very much relieved that we would not be going onto the ice as an airport.

Dead Caribou Bags Hunter

Keith. Options.

1. If you are not ok. lay down and spread eagle ⤳ & I'll have a chopper come in pronto. From Delta

2. There is a ridge in the trees up the hill - I may be able to land on. Right hand up. Maybe not. Another Cub pilot may be able too also. Commercial. 2nd best option i think

3. We can not find a float plane yet in Tok or Delta. But could in a few days if you just want to wait there. Cost. $200⁰⁰ or so. (Wave a Coat)
(Probably Best Option)

4. There is a chopper in Tok - but the pilot is away from phone today. ? Probably 1 hour chopper time if you do not have a bear. or Maybe if you do Both hands on head

⑤. Other option use signals on hunting licenses. OON

L(over) (Now)   Spike

Keith Evans

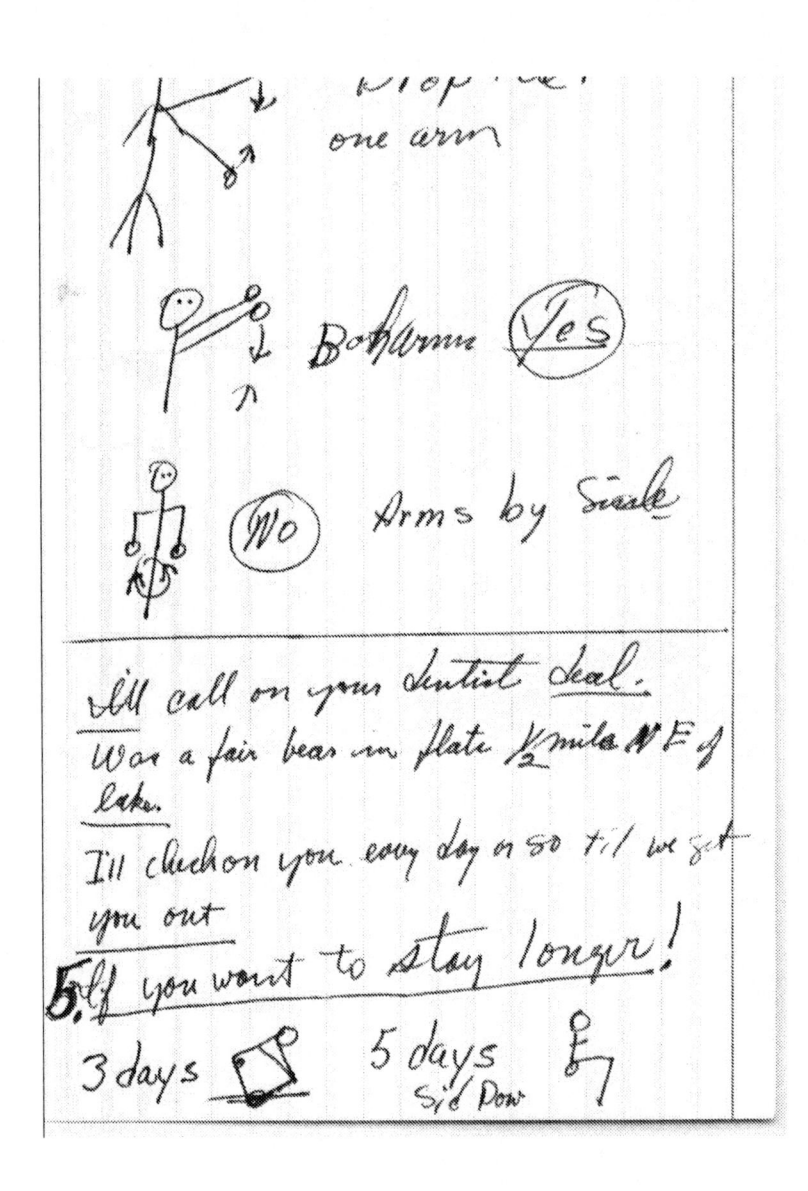

[handwritten notes with sketches:]

one arm

Both arms — Yes

No — Arms by Side

I'll call on your dentist deal.
Was a fair bear in plate ½ mile N E of
lake.
I'll check on you every day or so til we get
you out
5. If you want to stay longer!
3 days   5 days
          Sic Pow

Dead Caribou Bags Hunter

Figure 19 STOP AND SMELL THE ROSES.

    I relaxed by sitting in front of the cabin in a lawn chair. I remembered my mother's words, "stop and smell the roses." I decided I needed to do just that and really enjoy nature to the fullest. So I pealed off all my clothes, with just a long sock over my privates. I didn't want to embarrass any of the creatures that might happen by. I'm sure that wasn't what my mother meant, but the sun was so warm and it was a very remote place, besides I could use a nice tan. As I sat there I listened and watched more intently as to what was happening around me. A few houseflies were bothering me, so I decided to terminate them by clapping my hands together and catching them between them. That was a technique I learned a number of years ago and got quite good at it with lots of practice when the wife and I went on a sailing trip and got covered with them.

    Well, a few claps later and the flies were history. I dropped the flies on the ground. In being more observant, I noticed ants crawling around, as you would expect. No big discovery. However, what would the ants do if I dropped one of the flies next to them? I found one of the flies and dropped it next to one of the more aggressive looking ants. One ant grabbed the fly by its hind leg and began to pull it. I was amazed at the strength of the ant. He picked up that fly which was many times his weight and started carrying it over stones, limbs, and up and down grass stems. Another ant came along and decided he would help out, so he grabbed another hind leg and started pulling. No, not in the same direction, but in the opposite direction. I watched first one ant pull the fly and the other ant along with it over several inches of ground, and then the other ant would take over and do the same thing. Every once in awhile they would both let go of their leg hold and fight each other for a second, then grab their leg and continue their tug of war. I wondered what would happen if I dropped another fly beside them. Would they each take a fly and go their separate ways? I found the other fly and dropped it between the two energetic ants. They would not take a second look at the new donation. Maybe these two were just obstinent and not demonstrating usual ant behavior. I picked up the fly and dropped it in front of a smaller ant. He grabbed the fly and started hauling it away. After hauling it several inches, a larger ant came along and took hold of the fly and hauled it and the little ant back the way the little ant had come. What? Here comes another little ant. Reinforcements. The second little ant grabbed a leg on the same side as his small companion and the "war" was on. It was now about even. First the two little ants would gain an advantage, and then the single bigger ant would haul them over some ground. Every little while they would stop and tear into each other and then resume their tug of war. I got tired of watching. Is this what my mother meant when she said, "Take time to smell the roses?" These ants reminded me of some people I know. Once they get their mind set on doing something they fail to take advantage of a better deal, which comes along. Wow, twenty minutes of ant watching, mixed with swatting flies and watching the shoreline while looking for bear-bare, made for a pleasant afternoon.

    Tuesday, the 26th of May turned out to be another beautiful day. I got up early and decided to explore the little lake that was in the woods east of the cabin. I found some game trails and then hit a survey lane, which made walking easier. I noticed some bear droppings from earlier in the year, so I knew they used these trails. Spike had also said in the note he dropped that he saw a grizzly on the

Dead Caribou Bags Hunter

flats northeast of the cabin. If I was lucky I might happen onto one along one of these trails or along the little lake. It would be difficult in the woods, because I could not see very far. I found the lake and sat down on the bank. It was very peaceful. The seagulls were there in pairs and in some cases small flocks. Several came diving at me several times. Since there was not a nest in sight, I assumed they were just showing off for their mates who were perched on top of a stick. One of the most enjoyable sounds of nature to me, are loons "crying" to each other. A pair of loons were on the lake and were rather social. I heard them make several sounds, almost like purring, which I had not heard before. They swam over to a little island and walked up onto the ground, but still in the water. The male was rather impressive with his balance. It was hard to believe he could get on top of the female and be so upright and not fall off. It's amazing what can be done when there is enough incentive. I couldn't tell which one or if it were both, making the purring sound.

I sat there for about as hour watching the ducks, birds and muskrats. It was very relaxing and especially nice without mosquitoes flying around me. I thought there might be lots of them with such warm weather. I walked back to the cabin and made myself some soup and took it outside to eat. After eating I went back into the cabin and indulged myself in a time killing activity, solitaire. I won every time except twice. No, I played fair. There was nothing to read except a little first aide booklet.

Spike flew out that evening and dropped off some food and a fishing pole and reel, along with several artificial lures. I could now go fishing. He also indicated that the floatplane would pick me up tomorrow, Wednesday. I had seen several pike in the lake when I was in the boat down at the shallow end of the lake.

Wednesday afternoon the plane was supposed to pick me up. I packed up all my gear and put it in plastic bags and placed it on the shore in front of the cabin so I would be all ready to leave when the plane arrived. I hung around the cabin all day expecting the plane to arrive at any time. I was amazed that the lake was completely cleared of ice. For much of the day on Monday and Tuesday I had spent in the boat breaking ice and pushing ice flows around trying to make sure there would be enough open water for the floatplane to land. I knew that I was probably wasting my time and efforts, as the wind would arrange the ice however it wanted to. Now I didn't have to worry about the ice. It was all gone as a result of warm weather and wind. I was certainly glad not to have ice to worry about. My left shoulder had been aching for several days, and would continue to do so for about a month after this outing.

Two swans landed and were curious about my ice breaking and would swim up to within a 100 yards of me to watch. Probably thought I was some kind of nut.

During the afternoon I sat on the ridge in front of the cabin in the lawn chair, listening for an airplane. Now I don't know if you believe it, but sometimes you can imagine you hear things. Sometimes you do hear things that you mistake for other things. I did hear and see several planes fly past in the general area of the cabin over the past few days. You have probably heard that Alaska is noted for its huge mosquitoes. It's true! While sitting there in the lawn chair every day I had to become observant. You see, the mosquitoes sounded like airplanes, especially if there had just been one flying past. My first action was to look for a shadow. That's right, if I could see the shadow of the mosquitoes then I did not have to look up into the sky to see if a plane was there. It saved a lot of sky looking. The mosquitoes normally did not gang up on me. Maybe two or three at any one time and I could normally fight them off or kill them. As big as they are they are not real aggressive. They can however, be rather sneaky. I learned that it was best to leave my hat in the cabin and just wear my hooded sweatshirt. I got tired of chasing my hat. It is surprising how strong the mosquitoes are up here. They were not able to pull off my sweatshirt, however.

One thing that was truly amazing was the speed at which some of the ducks could fly. While sitting there on the ridge I kept searching the sky for jets. I could hear the swooshing sound of something traveling through the air at great speeds. Exactly like a jet sound. I was fooled time and again by the "jet sound", as it turned out to be ducks diving down to the lake or just going over it low. I started looking for the jet stream, but couldn't find any behind the ducks. They flew at tremendous speeds. One reminded me of an F-16 jets, the way it came straight down out of the sky. It was spectacular.

There was even more entertainment from the ducks. This hen mallard was such a tease. She would swim around the drake quacking and then fly a little ways away and land. The drake would fly after her and land beside or near to her. When he would start swimming toward her, she would take off again. This went on and on. I would have to believe that if she ever let him catch her he would be too tired to do her any good.

The floatplane did not come as expected on Wednesday. I carried my gear back up to the cabin for the night, along with some water for the evening and morning meals. More solitaire to kill some time.

Thursday morning arrived and I assumed that the floatplane would make it sometime today. It was such a beautiful morning. There was no wind and the sun was shining brightly. I took the fishing pole and decided to paddle across the lake to see if I could catch a pike. Spike had also indicated by a map in one of his notes that there were a pair of moose antlers along the bank of the creek that ran out of the lake at the east end. He said the owners of the cabin make jewelry out of antlers, so if I had time to get them, they would appreciate it. I paddled the boat across the lake and found the creek outlet. I hiked along the creek and found the two antlers lying side by side. They were probably a forty-inch spread on the head of the moose. I carried them back to the boat feeling good about finding them. As I paddled up the edge of the lake I looked for pike.

The fishing pole Spike dropped had been well used, with a piece of wire taped on to the tip in a big loop as the eye for the line to run through. The line on the reel was about 8 lb test. I put a steel leader on, attached a spoon and went fishing. It was a gorgeous morning. No wind, a clear sky and a warm sun. I wondered if the floatplane would get here today, knowing I would not make my dental appointment even if it did. Oh well, enjoy fishing. I threw out the lure and started rowing along slowly. I saw several pike following the lure, but none hit it. I changed to an artificial worm. On the first cast a large pike hit it and took off. The line spun off the reel until it stuck and snapped. I took the reel apart and fixed it and decided the line was a bit old and I would have to fight any other fish cautiously. The problem had been the line had become snarled on the inside of the reel. Since I had seen a spool of line in the cabin, which was 20 lb test, I decided to throw away the old line and replace it with some of the new. With that done I could fish with more assurance that I could handle a large pike.

Within a short time I had caught several pike that were in the 5 lb range. I decided to keep several for lunch. While fishing I was entertained by a group of ducks. They were splashing around, with the males chasing the females. That's typical this time of year. I had to smile at the vocal noise they were making.

I was finally very relaxed, even though I would not make my dental appointment which was scheduled for 10:00 am today. Catching pike and listening to ducks on this remote lake was much more enjoyable. Watching them mate and quack about it was preferred to sitting in a dentist chair getting oral surgery. Yuk! I would just have to make another appointment. I probably wouldn't be able to get one until the first of August. Let's see, that would be about time to hunt moose and caribou. Maybe I will be able to plan around the next appointment like I did this one.

Well, I decided I had better paddle back across the lake and fix my fish for lunch. I didn't need to pack, since everything was already and waiting, except for my sleeping bag, which I used last night. I slowly paddled back across the lake. When I was about 200 yards down the shoreline from the cabin and about 50 yards off shore, I looked up the shoreline beyond the cabin and there getting out of the water was a big black bear. He got out of the water onto the bank heading in the direction of the cabin. He disappeared into the evergreens covering the shoreline. I quickly paddled toward the cabin. I stopped after about a 100 yards and looked along the shoreline, as I continued to drift along. I was about 75 yards off the shore in front of the cabin. He came out from under an evergreen tree just below the cabin and looked directly at me. I slowly picked up my 375 mag, put the cross hairs on his shoulder and squeezed the trigger. He dropped where he stood. I wondered if this was the guy who broke the window in the cabin. I paddled to shore and walked over to the bear. Now instead of just two fish to fillet, I would have a bear to skin and cut up. No time to waste. I took out my knife and took care of the bear first and then did my fish.

Figure 20 Me and the cabin black bear.

Shortly after my lunch of pike, I heard a plane coming. I looked for shadows first and didn't see any so I knew it was really a plane. Sure enough, I was going to be leaving this lovely spot. We loaded in my gear and bear and arrived back in Tok about 5:30 p.m. After saying my "thanks" and "goodbyes" to Spike and family I headed back to Anchorage, 326 miles away. Being stranded for three extra days had its reward.

Keith Evans

FIVE GRIZZLIES IN HALF A DAY
ALEKNAGIK LAKE, AK.
5-15-93

Friday, may 14, 1993 was a nice sunny spring day and i looked forward to leaving after school to go bear hunting. I was in my truck at 6:45 p.m. After attending a head start graduation at the school. It was a long day. Oh well, i was going hunting. I was supposed to meet mark vingoe out at his place around 7:00 p.m. As i headed down the street, i was passing the high school when my truck started chugging and then it stopped. I used the starter to move it off the road to a parking lot behind the school. The last time it did that i waited a few minutes and it started back up. Unfortunately, it would not start again. I walked to the post office and came back to the truck. It still wouldn't start. I then walked home and called mark. He decided to come down to see if we could get it going. We tried to get it started with starter fluid and pulling it. No dice! We then hauled it to the garage and mark brought me home. He said, "carol needed the truck so we wouldn't be going hunting. At about 8:00 p.m. Mark called and said carol wouldn't need the truck and he would come and pick me up so i could stay overnight out there.

We got everything ready to go so we could leave early the next morning. Well, that's what i thought. I woke up at 5:00a.m., thinking mark was supposed to be up at least by 5:30. At about 6:00 he still was not up, so i went upstairs and went into his bedroom. He was still sleeping. I had to wake him. He claimed he didn't get to bed until midnight because renee, his daughter, kept him up.

We left about 7:00 and drove up to the end of the road at aleknagik. The boat was loaded and we headed down a smooth lake that was devoid of ice. The temperature was 40, but threatening of rain. It took about an hour and one half to get down the 20 miles to the end of the lake. We had stopped to check out a vacant cabin near the end of the lake, just in case we needed to stay overnight. It looked good enough for us. We saw a family of otters swimming along in front of the cabin as we were leaving.

At 9:30 a.m. We loaded our guns, grabbed day packs, and decided to hike toward the mountain on the north side of the lake. I no more than got started up the first hill, when my right knee hurt like hell. I had not twisted it, but it apparently got stiff riding all that way in the boat. I couldn't put any weight on it or straighten it out without it hurting. After some tender steps, it began to feel better. I decided to try and work it out. After about a mile over some rough terrain, i could walk fairly well without too much pain. We were near the base of the mountain and dropped our gear on a knoll in an open area. We glassed the mountain, which had snow on the upper part. We had something to eat and drink then continued glassing. I saw a bear about two miles down the mountain at the lower level. I took out my spotting scope and we could see him very clearly eating something. After a few minutes watching him, another bear came out of the brush and started eating also. We debated just a few minutes as to whether we should walk that far through a lot of alders to see if we could get into shooting distance. It was about 11:30 at that time. We decided to wait and see if we might find a couple closer. I looked up the mountain to our immediate right and spotted two bear up in the snow area. We decided to go after them. It was not going to be easy, even though they were a lot closer than the other two. It was now about 1:30.

We left our packs where we had dropped them and started crawling and climbing up the mountain. An hour later we were pushing through the last alder bushes after resting and climbing, climbing and resting. We were now in the snow. The bears had separated a little. The dark colored one had moved farther east on the mountain and the lighter one decided to ly down and rest. We decided to get in a comfortable prone position, take careful aim and shoot at the same time. They were at about a 45-degree angle up the mountain. The dark colored one was the one i was going to shoot and the light one was mark's target. I got ready to shoot rather quickly, but mark was having a hard time. I offered to shoot both brear or take a nap. He finally was ready. My shot flipped my bear over on it's back and it started sliding down the mountain and disappeared behind a ridge. Marks bear started running across the mountain. Mark yelled at me to shoot, which i did. It disappeard behiind the ridge. I got up and walked farther up the mountain beyond mark, while reloading my 375 mag. Just as i finished loading my gun, marks bear came over the ridge a couple hundred yards away running right at me. I could see some blood on his fur. I yelled at mark, "here is your bear.' he yelled back, "shoot him, i can't see him.' i raised my gun and just then it disappeared again, going down in a gulley. At that time the bear was about 50 yards away. I stood ready, not knowing where it would reappear. A moment later it appeared again, only this time it was about 20 yards away, coming nearly straight at me. I quickly took aim and fired. The grizzly dropped and slid. I decided to shoot again as it slid down the slope toward me. The bear came to a stop about 25 yards to my left. When it stopped, mark shot it again, just to be sure it wouldn't get up. It turned out that this bear was a beautiful blonde sow. She was not going anywhere, so it was now time to find out about my bear.

Figure 21 me after shooting mark's grizzly.

We walked over to the ravine and could see where my bear had made like a tobbogan, sliding around a horse shoe curve for about 500 yards. It came to a stop on an outcropping of stones, as if it had fallen there. We went down and inspected him. He was a dark chocolate boar.

Dead Caribou Bags Hunter

Figure 22 me checking my grizzlies teeth.

After about three hours of skinning we had both capes off, plus their skull, which we had to take to fish and game to get sealed. We also took some of the meat to try, even though you are not required to take the meat from grizzly bear. This was marks first bear ever, a nice one, at that.

We slid down the part of the mountain with snow and hiked back to our packs. The hides and skulls were heavy, and we were bushed by the time we got there, as going through alder bushes with a heavy load tires you out rather quickly. We decided to spred the hides over some bushes and come back for them tomorrow, as it was 6:00 p.m. And we didn't have time today to make two trips to haul hides and packs out. As we put our packs on we looked up the mountain where we had shot the bears and behold, there was another grizzly in the same area where our two had been. We blinked, and looked again. It walked around the area where we shot the bear, made a cirlce, then went back the way it had come. That made five grizzlies in a half day.

The going back to the boat was tough, even with only the day packs on. Two tired guys stumbling over uneven terrain finally made it to the boat at 9:30 p.m. What a relief. We had hunted all day in rain and were wet from it and from sweating. We looked forward to getting inside the cabin rather than setting up the tent.

We got the boat started and headed across the bay to the cabin we checked out on the way in. Most people will leave their cabin doors unlocked for emergency use. As we got near to the cabin we could see a boat on the shore in front of it. Damn, now what were we going to do. We were both cold and didn't really want to set up the tent. Wait a minute, what about minard's cabin down the lake farther. Let's check it out. We headed down the lake and when we could see chris and mac's cabin we were relieved that there was no boat in front of it, so we could use it. We beached the boat, unloaded our gear, went inside and got a fire going. After a hot cooked meal and getting out of our wet clothing, we felt almost alive. Our bodies were aching, especially my knee. It was swollen and tender. However, i didn't have any trouble falling asleep once into my sleeping bag. I was dead to the world in minutes.

I awoke at 6:30 a.m. And felt stiff. I got up and it was still overcast. However, it was not raining, so i considered it nice out and was ready to get going back for our bear hides and skulls. I waited until almost 7:00 and then made enough noise to get mark awake. He grumbled about sleeping some more. It was about 8:00 before i got impatient enough to roust him out. We ate breakfast of oatmeal and omelettes. Mark always brings everything, but the kitchen sink on hunting trips. We finally got headed into the woods at 10:00, in the rain.

Two hours later we were at the bear hides. I had brought along a plastic sled to haul the hides on. It belonged to mark and he thought it would make the job easier. We loaded the hides on and secured them. With ropes attached we headed through the alders and uneven terrain. After about one and a half hours of struggling and torment, mark said it was a bit too much to continue. We decided we would unload his hide and skull, since it was the smallest, and i would carry it on my back. Mark would pull the sled with mine on it. We started out again. Mark would pull and stop to rest. After a short ways, mark decided to rest awhile. I said i would haul his hide an skull to the boat and come back to help him. I went on and after an hour i was at the boat, having stopped to rest just three times. One of those times was to watch three moose feed in the river valley, which i started following. I dumped his hide and skull in the boat and headed back to mark. When i found him he had made it off the ridge and was coming along the river valley that i had followed. We both pulled the sled and finally made it back to the boat. It had taken us six hours for the round trip. We were drenched with sweat and the rain that never stopped falling.

It was four and we headed back to the cabin. Once there we put on dry clothes, cleaned ourselves up, ate, and cleaned the cabin. We packed the boat and headed toward the landing 15 miles down the lake. Fortunately, there was neither wind nor rain, so it was smooth going. We arrived at the landing about 6:30 p.m. In another hour we had driven the 25-miles back to mark's. We stretched the hides over some saw horses and mark took me home and picked up some salt. He took the next day off and fleshed out the hides and took the skulls out of the skin. The fish and game officer measured the skulls. Mark's was 21' and mine was 23'. A rough measurement of my hide was 94" across and 84" long. The taxidermist said it was an 8' bear rug. Mark's bear was a 7' size.

Keith Evans

THE BLUEBERRY DEATH MARCH
9-8-93

The long awaited hunt finally arrived. Scott and Clint Ball arrived Saturday, Sept. 4, and we planned on flying out to a hunting area in the afternoon. In making plans for the trip, it was hard to get a local charter with a plane large enough to carry our gear and us in one trip. We had a widgeon scheduled and then they cancelled due to mechanical problems. We finally had to make plan "B" arrangements due to bad weather and only the availability of a small plane.

Figure 23 Mac and Clint at Shannons Pond

A friend, Mac Minard, had a super cub, which he said would carry one person and a small amount of gear. He said the weather was bad where we wanted to go, Nuyakuk Lake, so he suggested we go to a friends cabin on a lake north of Okstukuk Lake. Caribou season would not open for a few days. Even though I was the only one able to hunt moose, it was agreed it was better than not going hunting. Mac took Clint and Scott to the cabin starting at 4:30 p.m. from Shannon" Pond, which is just outside of Dillingham. It was about an hours round trip per person. He was not feeling well after the second trip so he asked another pilot, Tom Johnson, who just returned from a charter, to take me up. He agreed, so we left at about 6:30. On the way up we saw six bull moose. Two were standing nose to nose. We also saw a black bear. Things looked encouraging.

While I was in route, Clint and Scott saw a large grizzly bear by the cabin and Scott took some video of it. They stalked it along the shore, over some small hills and through some alders. Things were getting exciting.

Figure 24 Grizzly checking us out as he ate.

The weather was windy and rainy, but we were determined to hunt and enjoy it. The next day, Sunday, we got up and looked in one of the sloughs and as we were paddling out we saw a grizzly on the shoreline. We sat and watched him and then paddled towards him. We could have saved some energy, as he decided to walk past us and over the beaver dam behind us—the one we just pulled the boat on. We paddled along the shore watching him catch floating dead salmon and eat the tasty parts. He didn't pay much attention to us. We followed him along the shore as he fished and ate until we came upon another bear standing in the trees by the shore. They were probably kin, as they walked into the woods looking back at us as they left. (See video)

Keith Evans

Figure 25 Grizzly feeding on salmon and watching us.

From there we tied the boat up along the shore and walked to several ponds next to the lake. I saw a bull moose, but he was not shoot able. We explored that end of the lake on foot because the waves were too high to use the boat. We made a big circle through the woods and came out a little below the cabin, farther away than I had expected. After getting something to eat we decided to go back down to the wind-protected end of the lake, near some ponds to see if the moose was around. Scott and Clint put their packs on and we left the cabin about 5:30 p.m. After tying the boat to a tree, we decided to sneak back to the pond and then to circle around, look at two other small ponds, and return to the lake. It was still blowing and raining. We walked down wind to the first pond and saw nothing. We walked crosswind for quite a ways and realized that we had not seen the other ponds nor were we at the lake. We saw a few caribou and sneaked up on them, as if bow hunting. We got within about 20 feet of two nice bulls. We walked up wind assuming we would find the lake. We didn't find it! We tried to figure our where we were in relation to the lake. I thought we had over-shot it, since we were trying to come back to the narrow end and just missed it. We then walked toward what we thought was the wide part of the lake, but no luck. The area was flat and wooded, so you could not pick out any landmarks. I should have followed my usual routine if lost, that being backtrack.

It was 9:30 p.m. and we had to accept the fact that we were going to have to make camp for the night. We found several young saplings and pulled them over and tied down the tops. It was still raining and blowing like hell. We found branches and wove them through the sapling tops we tied down to give us some shelter. We then put some evergreens on top of those branches and on the ground to sit on. Scott and Clint did a great job. They also gathered some wood. The dry kind was hard to find. They got a fire started after some effort. Everything was wet because it had been raining for the last two weeks. The birch bark took awhile to start burning, but once that got going the other wood gradually dried. Scott was very persistent. We should have made camp earlier so we could have gathered enough wood while it was light. As a result, we had to go looking for wood during the night with our flashlights. It was really a life or death matter, as hypothermia would have set in without the fire. We were all wet under our rain gear from sweating and or leaky boots. We could not find many pieces of wood that were burnable and would last very long. We had to use small sticks that would dry out quicker and would not put out the fire when placed on it. The fire had to be kept burning all night. I didn't get any sleep that night. It was cold and uncomfortable. That wasn't the only reason. My mind would not let go that I was responsible for what happened and I needed to figure out how to find the lake. I don't know how many times I tried to retrace our route in my mind. We later learned the wind-changed directions several times Sunday. If that was correct, instead of going up wind trying to find the lake, we were walking away from it.

Figure 26 Me cold and wet.

Keith Evans

Well, the first night was not pleasant. It was however, long. When we could see well enough to travel we decided to try to find the lake again. It was now Monday morning, another rainy and windy day with low visibility. We looked and looked, using compass bearings. We climbed trees, with no luck at sighting the lake. Scott thought it was in one direction and Clint thought it was in a different direction. We tried them all, but apparently did not walk far enough because at noon we still had not found the lake.

It was decided then that we were going to head due south – southwest and walk to the village of Aleknagik. We knew that no one would know we were missing from the cabin until late Tuesday afternoon when we were to be picked up. In looking at the map it appeared we could get to Aleknagek by Tuesday evening. Unfortunately, we were not at a cabin on a small lake south of Okstukuk Lake, we were at Braswell Lake where Leon Braswell had built the cabin we were staying in. We were north about seven miles of where we thought we were. We figured it was about 18 miles to Aleknagik. What we found out later was by snowmobile trails it was really 40 miles. Figuring a ground speed of about a mile per hour we thought we would be there by Tuesday night and call the charter person, Rich Grant and let him know we were safe. Unfortunately, things didn't work out that way. Mac Minard decided to drop in and see how we were doing and he determined we had been gone since Sunday because there was so little food consumed and the boat was swamped, still tied to the tree at the end of the lake. He immediately called his office (Fish and Game) by radio to alert them of his concern and to mobilize a search. We were well away from the lake by that time.

Figure 27 Scott looking at map and compass

As we walked south Monday afternoon by compass, our main concern was finding water so we would not get dehydrated. With all the water in the area, which we had seen from the plane coming in, we could not find any until about 7:00 p.m. that night. Clint had a dizzy spell prior to finding any, which concerned us all. We stopped and rested and ate some blueberries until he felt well enough to go on. We finally found the water in a small puddle and put some in a plastic bag for future use. We had six bars of food and some beef jerky Scott had brought along. By Monday night we had two bars left and a couple of small pieces of jerky. I didn't tell them I had a snicker bar and a granola bar in my pocket. I thought I would just save them in case it took us longer to get out than we planned.

We decided to stop earlier Monday night to allow more time to gather enough wood for the night and to prepare a shelter. Around 8:00 p.m. we found a big evergreen leaning on its side, with dead limbs on the high side. The water would naturally drain down the limbs and not on us. The wind was still blowing and it was raining off and on, like it had all day. We gathered wood, boughs and birch bark. A frame of limber sticks was put together around the evergreen tree trunk as a "shirt" to stop the wind. Scott again got his lighter out to start the fire. Sure glad he had that lighter. We would have run out of matches trying to get a fire started. We had some tense moments when no one spoke—only to himself—when the lighter quit working. We had no matches left. There was fluid and spark, but no flame. Scott shook it. He wiped off the flint with a tissue and it still didn't light. At that moment I was wondering if we could cut enough boughs and stay close enough together to prevent hypothermia. I didn't say anything. His lighter still sparked, but no flame. I don't know what he did to it, but it came to life with a flame—thanks old faithful lighter! Scott did most of the wood gathering. The pile was bigger than the first night. Once the fire got going good, we each tried drying out some of our clothes. Clint even went down to his undershirt. He got a little chilly. Boots came off and socks wrung out. Getting dry sure helped with the coldness. Once I put my head down, Scott said I was out. Don't know how long I slept, but it must have been several hours. You generally could not sleep very long because you would get too cold on the side away from the fire. I woke up to see Scott feeding the fire and then resting his head in his hands. Sometimes two of us would be up for awhile feeding the fire. On occasions all would be up trying to get warm. Scott looked for some game that night before we went to bed, but could not find any. We had seen small groups of caribou during our walk, but we didn't want to shoot one and take time away from walking. The night however was much more comfortable than the first. Clint did a good job of cutting off the wind by weaving sticks into a windbreak around the tree. The wind cools you down so fast that it's important not to have any hit you for very long, especially when you are wet. It was better for me personally because I slept and therefore felt better the next day. However, none of us got more than about three hours of fitful sleep.

Dead Caribou Bags Hunter

Figure 28 Scott trying to get warm by the fire.

The next morning at 8:00 we found the weather had improved. We were finally able to see some landmarks, the mountains. Clint, having come from several weeks on Outward Bound, became the navigator. He identified the mountains and let us know we were farther away than expected. It was nice to finally have a better idea of where we were. Even though it was bad news, as far as getting to Aleknagik that night. We pushed on with determination to travel as far as possible that day. The weather was nice but the terrain was a continual challenge, but worse was yet to come. We made a few rest stops. When we came to spot where berries were abundant we would stop for some nourishment and liquid supplement. The boys talked rather fondly of the blueberries.

During the day both Clint and Scott were feeling upset stomachs, nausea and of course tired. We stopped and drank water, rested and consumed berries. Then trudged on, as we had a ways to go. I was especially glad Scott decided he was able to walk farther Tuesday evening after a 25-minute nap. He had not been able to sleep the second night and it took its toll on him Tuesday. He lagged behind more and more so that was the reason we stopped to give him a rest. When I tried to wake him from his nap I yelled as loud as possible, calling his name. He didn't wake up. I had to shake him, which made me concerned. The boys decided that they could walk some more. Travel we did. We covered a lot of ground between 5:30 and 8:00 p.m. It made a big difference on our arrival time at Aleknagik the next day and also meant our energy level would be greater for the challenge we didn't know we were going to face. It would be the worst part of our walk.

We found a suitable place to build a fire that night and the rain stopped. It cleared up and got colder that night. We were more comfortable because we didn't have to contend with the rain and wind. The next morning we got started just after it got light. Yes, I did share the food I had in my pocket last night. We were running on guts, water and berries. Before getting to the largest patch of alder bushes I had ever been in, we crossed rivers and beaver backwaters. Each time we got wet. Clint and I had on hip boots that leaked and Scott had on regular hunting boots. However, the water was never more than knee deep. We started climbing into the alder jungle going up hill and across steep slopes. There was no other option. It began to rain, which added to the frustration of stepping over snake-like branches and bending under them, getting more water on our heads and necks. I muttered a number of choice words to myself as we progressed along our compass course. It seemed like we were never going to get out of that tangled mess. Finally we saw "daylight' and no more alders, just evergreens and tundra. We pointed toward a large hill, which would allow us to see our destination of Aleknagik.

Figure 29 Keith and Clint looking at village

Dead Caribou Bags Hunter

Figure 30 The three marchers relieved the march is over!

We trudged to the top of the hill, arriving about 2:00 p.m. What a sight to behold. The lake and especially the houses –civilization— it was gorgeous. There were a few yells and pats on the back, along with some picture taking. I was very surprised to see later that we looked rather fresh and good in the pictures. It was still necessary for us to decide where exactly we should go, as we still had an hour or so to walk to reach a phone. It was decided to head for the closest building. It was next to the private airstrip due southeast. It didn't look too far, but after an hour of going down hills and up hills, plus skirting alders, we arrived only to find no one home. However, there was a fellow at one place who was looking for someone. He had a foreign accent, so it was kind of hard to understand him. He did say that he came from a cabin just around the corner and up the hill, pointing it out to us. He indicated they had a phone. Off we went again. Several minutes later we arrived at the yard to see three guys moving foodstuff onto the porch. We received a warm welcome, even though they didn't know about our circumstances. They knew shortly. Jim Sanders, one of several guys who own the cabin, invited us in. What a nice guy. He had some food warmed up and three beers ready in minutes. All we wanted to eat and drink was available. It didn't take much, however to fill us up. Our stomachs had shrunk a bit. Jim mentioned that Pen Air was flying out to pick up a fellow at the private strip, which we had just walked down. I called Pen Air and asked if they had room for three more passengers. When I told the lady my name she asked me if I wanted her to call off the search.

I said, "What search?" She informed me that eight planes, a helicopter and two tracking dogs were looking for us.

"By all means, call off the search", I said.

It was now about 3:45 p.m. and the plane was due at 4:00. We had finished eating and I had cleaned up the dishes when the plane could be heard.

Jim said, "come on and we will give you a ride up on the four wheelers."

That was a welcome statement. We had all the walking we wanted for some time. A few minutes later we were saying

"Thanks and Goodbye" to Jim and his friends.

It was a short trip to Dillingham. When we got inside we were greeted by friends, Rich Dahlberg, Don Renfoe, Jeff Scrade and several others.

Pen Air said, "This trip is on us." Everyone was very nice.

We found out that the goose would bring in our gear, which had been left at Leon's cabin, from Fresh Water Adventures. Saved us the expense of going back for it. Unfortunately, someone decided to take my $200 binoculars. I still have not found them.

Mark Vingoe picked up the gear and brought it to us at my place. Mark and Carol were instrumental in helping with matters and worrying more than anyone else. Mark called family, Don Renfroe, Supt, and Gail and informed her we were lost. According to Mark she was not too concerned, having confidence we would find our way out.

Dead Caribou Bags Hunter

When we got back to my place we started taking off our well worn, wet clothes. The biggest surprise was when Scott took off his "waterproof" Browning boots. One sock was totally without a bottom. It was worn away completely. Scott's feet had the worst blisters of all. All our feet were white and wrinkled from being so wet. Blisters were the poached kind. My big toe and sole of my right foot still tingles and feels like it is asleep. We all showered and relaxed. Discussion took place about where Scott and Clint could go hunting before Friday to get Clint a caribou. It was decided they would fly up to Grant Lake Thursday and come back Friday morning. Some folks thought us crazy when they heard we were going back hunting. Scott and Clint left Thursday. Friday they got picked up and along with them came a nice caribou. (See Video)They stalked it and Clint shot it Friday morning about and hour before they were to be picked up. They got back during the late afternoon and we got his meat and horns packed. After a bite to eat we headed for the airport. Clint was off for Colorado at 8:30 p.m. One hunter leaving with a memory he will never forget.

Figure 31 Clint and his nice bull.

The Tough Are Persistent

Up to this point, Scott has not had a chance to hunt. He was getting a bit depressed, as the weather started getting rainy and windy again. We had planned on going up to Nuyakuk Lake on Saturday. Weather prevented it and Sunday was not looking any better.

Keith Evans

Saturday night we tried to allay our disgust by going hunting with Mark out by the dump. When Scott was flying Friday, they spotted several bulls a mile northwest of the dump. We had a long walk and Scott was pissed most of the way. We didn't see anything. Along about 1:00 p.m. on Sunday, our pilot, Tom Johnson, called and said he could take us. Scott loaded up and flew out. I would be the second load and would stop at Braswell Lake—cabin—to see if I could find my missing binoculars, dishes and other items, plus making sure things were left the way we found them. I left Shannon's pond and came home to wait until Tom returned from taking Scott. An hour or so later I loaded up and left with Tom. We stopped at Braswell Lake. I found some of our stuff, but no binoculars. We put things back in place and then flew on to Nuyakuk Lake. Tom said, "Scott saw two moose and told me to land." He said that if he were not at the tent site, he would be out scouting. Sure enough, as we approached the spot where Scott was suppose to be, we saw a bull moose about a quarter mile off shore, but no Scott. We landed and unloaded. Tom said, "so long, I'll see you Wednesday at noon, weather permitting."

I started setting up the tent and getting the camp organized. Thank heavens, it wasn't raining. I had just finished putting up the tent and got things organized inside when Scott showed up. He said he had seen a nice bull moose while he was out scouting. I half expected him to say it was over yonder dead. However, you are not supposed to hunt the same day you fly and he honored that law. We took another hike along with pumping up the inflatable boat and cruising the shore for about thirty minutes. As it turned out, we didn't need the boat. The wind came up and made it undesirable to use, even if we had wanted to.

We decided to hike farther back from the lakeshore on Monday morning. After we got back to the area where Scott had been Sunday night we decided to split up. Scott was going to head towards a divide between a wooded ridge and some open parks. I decided to walk down an open park and circle back along the edge of the woods Scott would be by. As I moved slowly along the parks edge I saw a cow and calf come out of the fog and rising sun. I backed into a tree and took out my telephoto lenses and got it set. They were on the other side of the park and directly in the sunlight. I took several pictures of them. They stopped when they caught my sent and turned directly away and went into the woods. I continued along the edge. What a nice morning. I was expecting to see a large bull step out at any moment. I kept walking along slowly. No moose. About an hour later I got to the spot where I expected to see Scott. He wasn't there. I stood there looking into the open park where I had started. Just then I heard the sound of antlers hitting tree limbs. After hearing the first sound, I thought, Scott's screwing around hitting a tree with a stick. However, listening to the sound some more, I decided it was too authentic. I turned toward the tree and brush covered knoll beside me. The sound was coming from the ridge of woods I had just circled. The moose was within 50 yards of me, but I could not see him. He continued to hit and scrape his antlers on the tree branches. I expected him to step out any at moment. My rifle was at ready, with thumb on the safety. Just then I heard a noise behind me. Turning, I saw Scott approaching. A big smile and thumbs up sign. He heard the same thing I did. He came over and I told him I would circle back around and drive him out. The wind was perfect to do it. I went back around the tip of the woods and started into the brush. I had not gone over 50 yards up the tree and brush covered ridge, when I saw a scrape. I walked past the scrape and looked up the slope directly at a moose. He had his eyes and ears on me. Between his ears were small spike antlers. He looked at me a minute, then turned and walked a few steps directly away from me. I grunted like a moose does. He stopped and looked at me again. I knew this spike bull could not have made the thrashing noise that I had heard. Just then, beyond the spike bull, a large set of antlers began to appear. A large bull was walking up the hill on the other side of the spike. The smaller bull walked off to the right and the larger bull stood looking at me about 25 yards away. I raised my gun and put the cross hairs on his forehead. Should I shoot him between the eyes? Just then he turned his head and looked in the direction the smaller bull had gone. "Oh my what a nice neck shot." I put the cross hair on his neck. "No," I came to push him out to Scott whom came all the way here from Hawaii. Just then the bull started in the same direction the smaller bull had gone. I was concerned they were heading out between us and not out into the open park, as planned. I moved to cut them off. I heard some branches break, but I could not see them. All became quiet. Then bang, bang, pause, bang. I climbed the hill and went down the slope to the edge of the open park. I could then see the spike bull standing out in the open park looking back in my direction. It then turned and trotted off. I got farther out on the edge of the park and looked down the park to see a nice big bull staggering. Scott was 50 yards down the opposite way. I was between them, but not in the line of fire. Just then it fell down. I stood there and watched him to make sure he didn't get back up while Scott returned for his pack. He got his camera out and began taking video.

Figure 32 Scott and a nice bull.

Scott had been videoing a legal bull before I had arrived. He was along the edge of the park. I did not see that bull. After I arrived and we decided our strategy to drive out the bull we heard scraping the tree, Scott said I no more than got into the woods, when a calf moose came out and then the cow moose charged directly at him. He said he waved his arms, hands and hat, but the cow came faster. Her ears were back and her hair was up. She was also making a very unfriendly sound as she stopped about 15 feet from him, between him and the calf. Scott was on the verge of wetting his pants or something similar. He didn't want to shoot her, but he didn't want to be trampled by that mad cow. Just then a calf ran off. The cow turned and followed it. Scott's bladder relaxed, just in time to prevent another episode of wet clothes. Just then, out of the woods came a bull, about 125 yards away. It appeared to be of legal size. Then out stepped a bigger one, which left no doubt it was legal. The smaller one was in the way a bit so Scott waited until it took a step, giving Scott a clear shot at the big one. He took careful aim and the 375 mag roared. The big bull dropped and then got back up. Two more shots hit it and it staggered and then dropped. Wow, what a few exciting moments. I was glad I did not shoot it earlier.

Figure 33 Me doing my job of dressing out Scott's moose.

It was now 11:30 a.m. Monday, Sept. 13. 1993. The work was about to begin. After taking pictures and video, it was decided I would dress out the animal and Scott would start packing. He took our packs and headed for camp to drop them off and to pick up our pack frames. It took him about an hour to make the round trip. At 7:45 p.m. that night we had the moose meat and antlers back in camp. Scott made a total of six trips and I make three. We were tired that night.

It rained and blew all day Tuesday, that night and the morning of Wednesday. I was concerned we were not going to get out Wednesday. In fact, I had taken out my air mattress and sleeping bag, got in the bag and was reading when we heard Tom coming in his plane. It was decided that Tom would haul me out with all the meat and then come back for Scott and the gear. He was going to drop Scott off on his way back at Grant Lake. He would hunt caribou there Thursday and get picked up Thursday night, weather permitting. He wanted a caribou and that was where he and Clint were successful.

Scott got up Thursday morning at Grant Lake and had a great time watching and videoing caribou. He spent 30 minutes getting videotape of them eating, sleeping, walking around and sparring. He finally picked out a bull and shot it. While he was packing it out he had an encounter with a moose. It seems he was walking by some brush, which was higher than his head, and up stood a bull moose that appeared to be 7 feet tall. It was grunting and walking out. Scott grunted—at least that was what he told me, but I wonder if he didn't have to change his drawers instead. Anyway, the moose walked out into the opening, then smelled Scott. It immediately headed back into the brush, much to Scott's relief.

While Scott was out having fun, I was at school during the day and at night, cleaning and cutting moose meat. My refrigerator was packed so full I had to put a chair against the door to keep it shut. Yuk!, blood drained out. I had left three quarters hanging in Rich Dahl berg's barn, which we gave away because we had no place to put it.

When Scott came in Thursday night with his caribou we had to take it out to Marks. Scott spent most of Friday getting his things organized and mailing back bags parcel post. It cost him $54. That was cheaper than paying for extra bags on the airplane.

When I got home from school Friday night we started packing meat. We went out to Mark's to get his caribou first and then to Markair to get more boxes. Damn, they were closed. We therefore had to use several boxes I had at home that were not leak proof. We estimated the maximum of 70 lbs. after using Mark's scales to pack the caribou. We decided to go to the airport early to weigh the boxes. When we got there we had to wait for the people to clear out on the incoming flight. Then we began weighing and repacking meat. More boxes were needed, which we found upstairs at Pen Air. We ended up with eight boxes of meat and the antlers, which were taped and tied together.

It pays to know people. I was able to use my mileage ticket, which a regular agent said I couldn't because there were not seats

Dead Caribou Bags Hunter

available for a saver award. I talked to the manager whom I knew and she fixed me up with no trouble. The other thing, which was very helpful, they didn't charge anything extra for the eight boxes of meat. Saved a big bunch of dollars there.

Well, we had worked up a sweat getting the meat ready. It had taken almost an hour and we were about to get on the jet. I was wondering if anything could be a problem now. We planned on leaving the meat in the airport freezer over night in Anchorage and take it over to the International Airport in the morning, when Scott had to leave. We arrived in Anchorage about 10:30 p.m. and walked over to the storeroom. The sign of the door said, "Freezer closed." Damn, what are we going to do now? I thought a moment and then decided to call the Barrett Inn. They had a freezer, which I used in the past. A call to them got an "OK/" Next, how to transport it? I knew a taxi could not handle it. I mentioned my concern to a friend, Jay Baldwin, who had flown in with us. He said, "if you will wait, I will pick you up with my truck once I get it from the motel". We were glad to wait. He even offered to let us use it the next morning to haul the meat to the airport for Scott's departure. We did not need it as we hauled it out in a barrowed van and the Barrett van.

Well, we got to the International Airport at 8:00 a.m. Saturday. We had purchased another meat box from the Barrett to transfer meat out of the non-meat box. We could not get all the meat in that box, so I had one package to take back home with me. Glad we came early, as the line was fairly long when we got there, but it was very long by the time we finished packing the meat. Scott had gotten a couple to move his gun case along in front of them to save his place. They were just about up to the counter when we finished. I was concerned about how much it was going to cost Scott to haul 8 boxes of meat, his antlers and gun case. As we were hauling the meat boxes a man came up with two boxes and his name on them said, "Lihue, Hi." Scott talked to him and they worked out a deal on the extra bags they each had. To our amazement, you could check two bags free, the next three would cost $45 each, the next three would cost $60 each, and the next three would cost $120 each. Had they had to pay that, they would both have been hurting. The gal at the counter worked with them and I believe it cost about $400 for the extra boxes. Well, we had done it. Scott was ready to get on the plane and head home at

9:00 a.m. We went up to the waiting area and waited and waited. It was now 10:30 and still no boarding. I said I have to go do some shopping, assuming he would be on his way shortly. We said our "goodbyes" and I left. After leaving I thought I had better call to see what was happening with his flight. To make a long story short, I picked Scott and "friends" up at 2:30 because their flight had been cancelled and rescheduled for Sunday morning at 2:30 am, Vouchers were given for lodging and food. I dropped Scott's two friends off and he and I went shopping for my cupboard. We boxed my food and mailed it.

Marshall French, a friend from Mt Village who worked as our computer expert, called me so we ate with him and then retired early. Scott stayed at the Eagles Nest Motel and got off to Hawaii at 3:00 a.m. Sunday. His meat arrived in good shape and was enjoyed, along with some stories. Was that a hunting trip or not?

Note; Thirty-two people volunteered during the search for us. They had as many as eight planes and a helicopter flying. Also, two dogs were used to track us, but they didn't go far. Several weeks later at a parent open house meeting at school, the president of the PTA gave me a ball of string and the next time I went hunting she wanted me to tie one end of the string to the tent pole and the other to myself. When I got to the end of the string that was as far as I was to go.

Dead Caribou Bags Hunter

CARIBOU HUNT
DILLINGHAM, ALASKA
FEBRUARY 7, 1993

We had been talking about going up river to hunt caribou for the past several weeks. Reports from friends at Ekwok and farther up-river were amazing, because thousands of caribou were being seen. It took two and a half days of steady movement before the herd moved across the river at Ekwok. They were throughout the village and on the airstrip.

Rich Dahlberg, special education director at Dillingham City Schools, said the weather was supposed to break and get warmer this weekend. It has been −30 for the past several weeks.

Mark Vingoe was suppose to go with us this weekend, but Carol, his wife, was on jury duty and unfortunately he had to work on the case Saturday, 2-6-93. He gave us the key to Southwest Region's house at Portage, in case we went that far to hunt and wanted to stay over night. Vince Luckhurst, custodian at the elementary school, was going to go, but he had to take his son to Anchorage. He allowed me to use his snow machine, sled, and some gear.

Friday, 2-5-93 saw me getting my stuff together after school and going out to Riche's to get things ready. Vince brought his machine and sled over and we got things loaded up. We took several five-gallon cans of gas, plus survival gear, food, etc.

I got up Saturday morning at 6:00 a.m. and had a leisurely breakfast. My video camera and 35 mm were packed. I was hoping to get video of a lot of caribou. When I went outside to load the truck, I found it to be clear and cold. We later found out it was −30 that morning when we left.

I unplugged the block heater on my truck and started the truck and headed for Riche's. We topped off the gas in the tanks on the machines and left Riche's house about 7:15 am. Rich led the way out via a trail behind his house. We headed cross-country. I was telling myself that I was glad he knew where he was going and was glad he stopped before we had gone very far. My fingers were freezing. I had on a pair of insulated gloves, but they were totally inadequate. Rich said for me to grab the controls on his machine, since they were heated. I could hardly feel my fingers, especially the tips. They started to tingle and hurt as they warmed up. In a few minutes I was ready to go, but this time with my hands inside a pair of beaver mittens, which Rich had dug out of his supplies. I had already gotten a beaver hat from him, which was covering an army surplus hat, Mark had given me. Over both hats I had my fur-lined hood. The only things that got cold were my face and fingers. Rich gave me a facemask, which covered my nose and lower face. I had to put the beaver mittens up to my face a number of times to warm it up. After we started up from our warming stop and traveled several miles, Rich stopped again and said he screwed up and had taken a wrong turn. There were machine tracks going in all directions, so I understood how that could happen. We made several wrong turns before we got to Wood River. It was bumpy, with ice protrusions, which we had to go around or over. We crossed Wood River and headed across the tundra. As we neared the Nushagak River we found ourselves running along a ridge. Rich decided to go off the ridge down to the river. He looked down the steep, snow-drifted bank, with a line of brush at the bottom. Rich turned his machine around and edged up to the bank. He decided that his chance of getting down without trouble was not a good one. Fortunately, he has reverse on his machine. He backed up and selected another spot. Over the edge he went. The snowdrift was hard packed, almost like ice. He started to brake and his sled slid sideways, over taking him. It's runner dug in on the downhill side and flipped over. Rich had enough weight and speed to pull it forward until he hit the first brush. He stopped and righted his sled and drove the next few feet to the rivers ice. I was a bit apprehensive, to say the least. Not having ridden snow machines that much I did not feel that confident. I decided I would try to go down a bit slower, using the break. The slope of the bank was such that it fell away to one side, which meant you needed to go fast enough to keep the sled behind you or it would slide sideways. Well, I wasn't thinking about it sliding. Over the bank I went. Rich stood on the ice watching. Down the bank, brake on and the machine starting to slide sideways. The next thing I knew, I was off the machine bouncing across the hard packed snow. The sled caught a runner as it slid sideways, jerking the rear end of the machine downhill. It stopped. The machine was facing uphill with the sled sidewise. I picked myself up and climbed back onto the machine. It spun and wouldn't move when I gave it the gas. I had to pull the machine so it was facing downhill and then it pulled the sled out. The remainder of the short downhill ride through the brush went without incident.

Figure 34 The open tundra we crossed.

We headed along the Nushagak River and again out onto the tundra. We saw a couple of moose in the brush as we drove along. They would look at us and take a few steps and watch some more. At about 11:30 we reached the area where it was legal to shoot caribou. I was surprised that we had not seen some earlier, as there were lots of tracks across the river and on the tundra where they dug the snow for grass and lichen. We stopped and watched four caribou walk and feed across in front of us. They were too far to shoot, so we decided to split up. Rich would go around in front of them. I would go behind them. There were some woods behind them and they decided to head through the sparse part as we headed after them. The going was tough for me as the ground had big humps and drifts. I got half way across only to get hung up and the machine quit. The caribou were in the open tundra now about 400 yards or so away from me. They were looking back at us. Bang, bang, bang and bang, Rich had opened up on them. I sat and watched. It appeared he had hit one, but it kept going. All of a sudden, for what reason I don't know, the caribou turned around and started back the way they had come. Bang, bang, bang and bang. Rich emptied his gun again. However, all four of the caribou were down now. He drove up to them and shot those that were not dead. Rich then drove over to me and we got the machine off the hump that got me hung up. I drove toward the caribou and then looked back to see Rich still back there where I had been stuck. He had a towrope out and had attached it to his sled. Seems he had not been able to pull his sled while it was attached to his machine. I learned something new. He moved his machine to the next hump and was, by the use of the rope, able to pull his sled away. Little did I know at that time that we would need that rope, plus a longer piece, several times before getting back home.

Now the work was to begin. We got out our knives and Rich began to butcher one and I removed my coat and headed for another one. We got started slowly. Rich was having trouble cutting off the head of the one he was working on. I began to cut the head off mine. As I pushed down on the knife handle, with the blade facing up, I cut the jugular and blood squirted all over my hands and knife handle. My hand slipped down the blade and my thumb caught the cutting edge. It sliced a nice cut along the inside surface. Well, the blade was sharp. My blood mixed with the caribou's. I stuck my thumb into the snow, but decided that wouldn't stop the bleeding. Do caribou have HIV? No, but with all the concerns about mixing of blood, the thought went through my mind. I continued to dress my animal.

After cutting the tongue our for Vince, I started on the second one. Rich came over a bit later after "chewing off" the head of the caribou he was dressing. You have to find the joint behind the head; cut away all the connecting tissue and then bend the neck to "pop" it loose. We finished dressing out the animals and cleaned up our hands. Rich fixed me up with a couple of band aides for my thumb. We also had a drink of "hot" cider. I was glad that I ate a chocolate bar before we started to butcher because I didn't eat anything else all day. I decided trying to eat a frozen sandwich wasn't worth the trouble.

Prior to going after the four caribou I had gotten out my video camera, which I had kept on the snow machine seat between my legs, to keep it warm, only to find it would not work because it was too cold. All that trouble for nothing. I should have known better. I did take several pictures with my 35 mm. However, it was disappointing not to have gotten some video.

Dead Caribou Bags Hunter

Figure 35   Beautiful scenery and easy traveling.

It was early afternoon and the sun was brightly shinning. A native trapper had stopped and told us that he had seen about 200 caribou about 5 miles away along a ridge we could see from there. We had also seen a small herd just beyond the spot where we were, at the time we talked to him. We decided it would be fun to go see 200 caribou and I would shoot one if we could get close enough. After loading the four caribou on Rich's sled we headed out. We had not traveled far before we saw two caribou out on the tundra. There were lots of trails and digging in the area so I expected to see many more caribou. Rich dropped his sled and we decided to drive after the two who had departed away from us. As we topped a slight rise we could see the two watching us. It's funny to watch them. Just as they start to run, they leap up into the air and then start trotting. As we moved further out onto the tundra, I saw a herd bedded down. There were 20-30. As we approached they stood up and started milling around. Several trotted away. I stopped my machine and turned it off. The closest one was about 300 yards or more away. He stood broadside. I knelt down and rested on the hood of the snow machine, lined up the cross hairs on his shoulder and squeezed the trigger. He turned and trotted in a small circle and dropped. Another one to dress out.

Figure 36 The last one to dress out.

We drove over and found he still had a horn on one side. We had gotten four bulls and one cow. As we dressed him out Rich said the heart was not worth keeping because I had blown it apart. I felt good about the shot. What I didn't feel good about was that my trigger guard was loose at the end that holds the clip. I had to push it in, in order to chamber a cartridge from the clip. I thought about having a grizzly charging me and not being able to chamber another round. Didn't know what the problem was, but knew it would get fixed.

We had five caribou and the sun was still high in the sky. We loaded my caribou onto my sled and we drove the quarter mile back to Riche's sled. He got it hooked up and we headed toward the river, following a snowmobile trail. Rich was leading the way and after following the trail a mile or so Rich turned around and backtracked. He went a short ways then picked his way out to the river ice. It was fairly smooth going so we made good time.

Figure 37 Snow and frost covered bushes and trees.

It looked like we would get home before dark. As we approached the fish camps along the ridge above the river, we could see water on top of the ice between us and the steep hill over which the trail went. The ice in this area had been broken and pushed up in pieces so you had to travel slowly. As we approached the waters edge, Rich stopped and shut off his machine. We noticed five other snowmobiles down the river on the bank. The riders were off their machines standing on the bank. Rich walked down and talked to them. While he was walking back they got on their machines and drove up river to the fish camp and came down the trail and crossed over the water-covered ice. There was only about ten feet of water-covered ice, but you couldn't tell how deep the water was on top. Rich fired up his machine and went across. The ice protrusions were so rough that he could not go fast enough to get up speed to get over the hill. It was ice covered. Now what were we going to do? I got on my machine and crossed the water, stopping behind Riche's machine. We decided to unhook the sleds and see if we had enough rope to reach the top of the hill. He went up as far as the rope reached and hooked up the sled. We couldn't move the sled. His machine just spun. The other guys were still across the river, so Rich called to them asking if they had any rope. Two of them came across with a rope. It was attached to ours and Rich drove to the top of the hill. We had dropped off two of the caribou from his sled to lighten the load. What I didn't know while all this was going on, was that a five gallon can of gas that was in the front of my sled had turned over and the cap had come off. The whole five gallons had drained into the sled. The caribou was on top of the tarp, which was under and over my bag containing my clothing and sleeping bag. The neck of the caribou, my clothing and the cover over my sleeping bag would all be contaminated. We put the empty can on top of my sled and went to work getting Riche's sled over the hill. He pulled it up ten feet and then lost traction. We had gone far enough to give back the rope we had barrowed so the five could be on their way hunting. We told them where to look for the caribou and thanked them for their help. They left and we went back to the task of getting the sled up the rest of the way. We pulled it up five to ten feet at a time. Finally it was up and over. We tied the rope on the caribou, one at a time and pulled them over. Next, came my machine. We detached the sled and Rich road it over the hill. The rope was then attached to my sled. We had to hand pull it about 15 feet in order to attach the rope to Riche's machine. He didn't have any trouble pulling it up the hill. I walked up. I felt like I should have asked Rich to hand the rope to me so he could pull me up. I was hot and tired of pushing; tying and untying knots to hoist up the sleds and caribou.

We reloaded the caribou and reattached the sleds to our machines. It was now 5:45 p.m. and getting dark. Now we could head home without any more problems. The going was bumpy and slow across the tundra because of the sparse snow in some areas. We had some smooth going on the river ice and in general, were making good time. Rich would periodically turn around to see if I was still coming and to give the thumbs up sign to keep going. I would signal the same sign back.

We approached a river, which we had crossed on the way out. It was one of the several small streams that are tributaries to the Nushagak River. This one had water covering the ice. Rich got off his machine. There was about twenty feet of water to cross, but how deep was it? I went and got a stick from a bush and measured the water depth out as far as I could reach. It was about 8" deep. Since we did not have much of any option other than crossing it, Rich fired up his machine, put it in low gear and went across. The water flew and for a moment his sled tipped and I thought it was going over. I could imagine trying to right it standing in water on the ice. He made

Dead Caribou Bags Hunter

it up the bank safely. I started my machine and felt more confident, since my load was lighter. Down the bank, through the water and up the bank, with only a moments scare, as my machine spun for traction.

On we went. Another river to cross, but it was smaller with only about ten feet of water to cross, but there were big pieces of ice to negotiate around. I was concerned about traction, but we both make it safely.

It was dark as we drove along the ice covered Nushagak. We crossed over to the Wood River and threaded our way through ice outcroppings. We started up the bank and it was pure ice. Rich couldn't get enough traction to get over so we got out the rope again. Tie and untie. Move a few feet and repeat the operation until we were over the bank. Fortunately, I had a longer run and made it up without help. We kept on going. The lights of Dillingham had been visible for some time. It just seemed like we were not getting to them very fast.

It appeared we were about ready to mount the bank of the Wood River and cut across the tundra to Riche's house. What do you suppose we faced? Another steep hill, which was ice. Rich could not pull his sled up so we got out the rope and with one short pull after another we got his sled up. We were getting good at it. We certainly should, after so much practice. I made it up without help and we were again on our way. We cut the road by Nerka subdivision and took it to a trail running along a power line to Riche's house. It was now about 8:30 p.m. We had been on the machines for a bit less than 14 hours and covered about 80 miles.

Rich opened his garage and we drove through, dropping off my caribou and Riche's sled loaded with his caribou. We would hang the caribou tomorrow, Sunday, 2-7-93

I was sore. Deborah, Riche's wife, had some supper for us. So after eating I came home and took care of gas smelling clothing, showered and went to bed. Wow, what a day.

Keith Evans

THE INVASION FROM HAWAII
AUGUST-SEPT. 1994

Son Scott brought Pat and Mike, brothers, plus another friend, Frank from Hawaii, to spend a couple weeks hunting in Alaska. Scott met them through his two businesses on the island of Kauai. His long time friend, Clint Ball, from Colorado, would also be with them, but only for the first week. I would be able to hunt the weekends.

Arrangements were made with Freshwater Adventures at Dillingham airport to fly the five guys and gear to a remote lake for some hunting. The goose was filled with gear and hunters as they departed the airport. About 45 minutes after take-off, they arrived at the lake and unloaded their gear. Where to set up their tents? "Look over there," said one of the guys. He was pointing at a wooden platform built on the tundra just off the beach. Since it was public land, they decided the deck would be a fine spot to erect their tents. Once that was done they inflated the zodiac boat I had borrowed form my friend, Mark Vingoe.

Two days later they heard a plane coming toward them. It landed on the lake and taxied right up to the beach in front of them. Out climbed three guys. The youngest looking one walked up to the five guys looking at him and introduced himself as a guide working for Bristol Bay Outfitters. He said they were responsible for the deck building and that over in the brush was an 18-foot Lund, which was also theirs. Fortunately, he was smart enough to know that he could not force Scott and friends off the deck and graciously went down the beach to set up their camp.

The first day of the hunt the guys went down to the end of the lake. They beached the boat near a semi open area on the bank. After climbing through some alders, they were just getting to the top of a small ridge when they spotted some caribou. Pat and Scott were together and it was decided that Pat would get the first shot. There was a nice bull standing a short distance away. The bull had a nice set of antlers, which were in velvet. This would be Pat's first caribou. Bang! Bang! The bull stood a moment and then dropped. The other caribou with it just slowly walked away, as they walked over to the dead bull. They had no fear of the shots or them.

Pat was all smiles. They were all happy because they only had about 150 yards to pack the meat and antlers to the boat. After that job was done they all headed up drainage to see what they could find.

They walked along an open ridge overlooking the large drainage and saw several caribou, but they were too far away to shoot and too far to go after. Finding animals as close as possible to the boat was a prime consideration. They topped a small knoll and there, walking along the brush line, but in the open, was a single bull caribou. Scott had his bow and he needed to get close for a good shot. He bent down and slipped around a knoll to cut off the bull. When the bull passed he decided not to shoot because the shot was not a good one.

Frank, who also had never shot a caribou, had a chance at this one. It was out of Scott's range, but not his. He clicked off his safety as he knelt, took careful aim and shot. The caribou staggered. Frank shot again and it went down. After congratulations and playful ribbing, they dressed it out, cut up the meat and hauled it to the boat. That was it for the day.

Figure 38 Frank's nice bull caribou.

The next day, Scott with his bow, Mike, and Pat with the video camera, headed out together. They took the zodiac part way down the lake and decided to climb a small ridge running parallel to the beach and then parallel with the drainage area. They climbed through the brushy area along bank and were climbing up the ridge on open tundra, when Scott spotted a bull caribou ahead. Since Scott had his bow, they needed to get close to give him a good shot. He and Mike bent down low and moved behind a small hill between them and the caribou. As they topped the hill, Scott stood up and brought his bow to full draw. The caribou, now three bulls, saw them and started running away. Scott didn't want to chance a poor hit, so he let off on his draw. Mike shouldered his rifle, took aim and "click." Expletive! He had not chambered a cartridge. He racked a cartridge into the chamber and fired. He was about to fire again when Scott coached him by saying, "wait, wait until it stops, now." Mike shot not just once, but three times. He got a nice bull. Pat, all the while was recording this on video, just for the record. Two smaller bulls trotted off. They again were lucky, as they had a short pack of about 100 yards to the boat.

When they got back to camp they found Frank scrubbing himself in the lake. He said he couldn't stand how he smelled, after doing all the work hauling meat and walking the tundra. They all agreed he did smell better after lathering up good with soap and a rinsing in the cool lake.

On the third day, which was cloudy with light rain periodically, the guys spotted two bulls just off the lakeshore, with not much cover to sneak behind. About one and a half hours later of careful sneaking, Clint put his crosshairs on one of the bull's front shoulders and Pat did the same on the other bull. The bulls were standing about 200 yards away, but they decided they could not get any closer without scaring them. Bang. Bang. Both bulls went down. Clint's bull was not as big as the one he shot last year, but it was of respectable size. The antlers on his bull still had some velvet left on them. Whereas Pat's bull had rubbed all the velvet off his antlers. Pat's bull was a lot larger than the first one he shot. Lucky guys—another short pack back to the boat.

I flew out on Friday to find a happy camp of guys. Scott and Frank were just getting back to camp after each shooting a caribou some distance away from camp. Pat, Mike, and Frank had their licenses filled for caribou and Scott and Clint each had one. The guys were all kind of tired, but I was anxious to hunt, so I headed out with my 375 mag for a look around. I walked just off the shore up a ridge behind camp and then cut up the edge of drainage. As I left a wooded area, heading up a hill toward open tundra, something caught my eye.

I looked to my right at trees and brush and I could make out the antlers and head of a nice bull moose looking directly at me. There was brush in front of his face and as I was deciding if I should chance a head shot through the limbs, he made up my mind for me by turning and disappearing in the trees. I took several steps toward the area where I had seen him and there appeared the dark body of another bull. Before I could raise my gun to shoot, he too disappeared. I then climbed higher on the open tundra hoping to see them again. They stayed well hidden because I never did see them again.

Figure 39 Blonde grizzly on front feet looking at me.

I walked farther up the hill and had just rounded a small patch of brush. I looked to my right across the tundra. What was that laying on the open tundra about 30 yards away? There, apparently sleeping was a blonde grizzly bear. I took off my pack and found my 35 mm camera. I somewhat reluctantly put down my rifle and raised the camera to my eye ready to take a photo. I then yelled, "hey." Nothing happened. I yelled again. This time the grizzly rose up on his front legs and looked at me. I took several quick shots. He then stood on all fours and lowered his head to the ground. I took several more pictures. Then he started eating blueberries. Either he didn't know what I was or he didn't care. I wondered what he would do if I walked out on the tundra upwind of him. I put the camera in my pack, put the pack on my back, picked up my rifle and slowly walked upwind. Of course, I watched him closely with every step. He would

Keith Evans

look my way, but he kept eating berries. When I got directly upwind of him, he raised his head and I could see him sniffing the wind. He turned and took several steps away, fed some more and then repeated that same thing until he had reached a ditch about 200 yards away. There he turned and looked in my direction and walked into the brush. I think this was the same bear that I will tell you about later on this hunt. I went back to camp with something interesting to share.

The next morning we all hiked back up to where I had seen the moose and the grizzly. We didn't see the moose, as they must have left the wooded area we had just "combed" on our way up. We climbed to the top of the hill overlooking the drainage. We saw some caribou at the far end of the lake and a cow moose with her calf heading down the drainage toward the lake.

Figure 40 Scott and his bull.

Scott and I walked on the backside of the hill while the others kept glassing. As we were topping a knoll, several bull caribou took off running. I shot, thinking I hit one, but it went behind a knoll. Scott could see it so he took my rifle and shot it. A long pack was in order, but with six guys there wouldn't be that much for each to carry.

Scott and I decided to take a different route back to camp than the others. We wanted to see of the blonde grizzly we had glassed while sitting earlier was still around the gut pile of the caribou shot earlier in the week. We walked down off the hill and were following a game trail and had just topped a small hill when we saw the blonde grizzly feeding on the caribou gut pile. We walked to within several hundred yards watching him eat. We stopped to video him. For some reason he took off running for about a 100 yards away from us. He then turned around and looked back toward the gut pile and us. He looked for just a moment or two and then walked back to the gut pile. I guess he decided he was in charge. Maybe he had smelled us from a stray breeze. He stood looking around beside his ready meal. We decided to wave our arms and see what he would do. The camera was going and we waved our arms to see what would happen. He took one look at us and took off running, huffing with every jump. He ran across the drainage and out of sight.

We think that Scott and Clint saw the same blonde bear on the gut pile of my caribou when they climbed to the top of the same hill to pitch their tent for an overnight spike camp. They saw the bear in the early evening feeding on the gut pile about 300 yards down the hill from their tent. They watched it eat for about an hour and then it layed there resting and even rolling with its feet up in the air. They hoped he would be satisfied with his meal and would not come near their tent that night. A very heavy fog rolled in that night and stayed until the next day. It made for a spooky night and morning. When they could finally see, they saw the bear sleeping on his back, next to the gut pile about 150 yards away. He didn't. Choose to investigate their tent, he was full.

Sunday afternoon Tom Johnson came to pick up Clint and me. Clint had to go back to Colorado and I had to go back to work for Dillingham City Schools. The four hunters left in camp decided they wanted to check out another lake nearby for a couple of days. They took one four-man tent and minimum food and had Tom fly them to Tikchik Lake.

The set up camp on the beach and went moose hunting. It didn't take long before they saw what they were after. They had walked into the evergreens covering the rolling hills adjacent to camp, for about 15 minutes when Mike saw a dark object behind some trees. He moved a little to his right and there between two trees was a bull moose looking at him. It then moved behind some evergreens just as he was raising his rifle to shoot. Mike stood still hoping the moose would continue walking toward an opening about 50 yards away. Bang! Bang! The moose went down and would stay down. Mike walked over and said, "I got bull winkle." He was still in velvet and had the three brow tines necessary to be legal. All the guys helped dress him out and pack the meat back to the camp just a short distance away.

What to do now? All licenses were filled, so it was time for a game on the beach. Mike would be the equipment manager. Pat would be the video camera man. Scott and Frank would be the participants in a two-man ball game. They fashioned a ball from pieces of material from their junk bag and used dried sticks that had washed up on shore for their bats. Needless to say, there was a running commentary from the two participants as to strikes and balls. The pitcher was always yelling, "strike' and the batter was yelling, "ball." They would switch positions periodically, supposedly after three outs. On one occasion Scott swung and the stick (bat) flew out of his hands and sailed into the lake. On another, Frank swung and the stick broke in half. Mike, of course, had to find them another stick. Scott was at bat and he hit a long one and ran around the bases while Frank ran to retrieve the ball. Frank got the ball and raced back and dove to touch Scott as he reached home plate. There was then a difference of opinion as to whether he was safe or out. That turned into a wrestling match with Scott ending up on top. He therefore declared himself safe and the winner.

Once back at base camp the guys were busy cleaning up their antlers by cutting away flesh so they would be ready for shipping. Scott went out in the boat early in the morning on a solo hunt. As he was arriving back at camp, he saw Mike on the beach with his rifle. Frank had been sitting just below the meat pole on the bank sloping down to the beach. Mike had just finished doing his chores of washing dishes in the lake and turned around looking behind him in the direction of the tents. He was stunned at what he saw. The head and chest of a grizzly bear was sticking out of the tall grass and bushes just in back of Frank.

Mike said, "ah Frank—bear, Frank—bear.' Frank looked up and started to move away. With a bit of yelling the bear moved back into the alders between the shore and the tent.

For the next several hours the bear would move back and forth from the tent to the meat pole trying to get something to eat. The guys would yell whenever the bear got near the meat pole. The bear then moved closer to the beach. Scott and Mike were on the beach and Scott looked up towards the tent and just to the right side, looking out of the tall grass was the blonde grizzly bear. Scott slowly bent down and picked up the video camera that had just been in use. When he looked back toward the bear, he had disappeared. Scott stood still trying to see where the bear might have gone.

Scott then said, "Mr. Bear, we don't want you in camp." "Go away Mr. Bear."

The bear's head came up again, looking directly at Scott. The bear then disappeared into the brush and could be seen moving brush as it went behind the tents. In just a minute it appeared coming down off the bank onto the beach, beyond where the meat hung in the trees. It was about 30 feet away and turned toward the guys with his nose to the ground. He swung his head back and forth smelling.

Scott kept the camera running and as the grizzly took steps in their direction, he said to Mike, " Put a shot right in front of him, but don't let it ricochet into him."

Mike took the 44 pistol and fired a shot, which kicked up sand in front of the grizzly. He stopped with a jump back. He then took several steps forward heading toward the guys, with his head moving back and forth.

"Put another one in front of him," said Scott to Mike.

Another shot was fired and sand flew again. This time the bear turned around and took several steps back. He again turned and headed back toward the guys. A third shot was then fired and this time he turned and walked up the bank into the brush. Where was he going now? They could see the brush moving as he walked behind the tents and started up the ridge. In a few minutes he was clearly visible, as he was sky-lined as he walked along the top of the ridge

Keith Evans

away from camp. The video was shut off with a comment, " there goes a problem bear." This was a long day.

    I flew in for a final day of hunting. I was looking for a moose. Frank said he would go with me for an evening hunt that late afternoon. We decided to take the zodiac across the lake near the outlet and check out the slough that was there. We motored over and entered the slough, but there was nothing but tracks. We decided to climb the adjacent hill for a good view of the entire area. We climbed to a flat ridge just below the very top of the hill, as to go to the top would have meant going through about 30 yards of alders. Besides, the ridge gave us a great view of everything we wanted to see. We sat there and glassed for about an hour. It was getting dim out. I happened to turn and looked behind us and there on the top of the hill walked a grizzly bear. He was sky-lined. We watched him walk away from us for about 50 yards and then he stopped, turned around and headed back the way he came. He had covered about 30 yards back when he turned abruptly into the alders coming directly at us. We could see the alders shaking as he bulled his way through. If he kept coming in that direction he would hit an open game trail leading directly to us. We stood up and faced him. He hit the open game trail and was about 20 yards away. We threw up our arms and yelled. He stopped. The hair on his back stood up. He looked directly at us and then he stood up looking. We yelled and waved our arms. He dropped to all fours and turned to his right going into the alders. We could see him going down the hill around us because of the alders shaking. We didn't see him again as he got out of sight at the bottom of the hill. We did however, watch for him very carefully as we walked down off the hill through some alders at the bottom. When we got back to camp, needless to say, we had another story to tell.

    Another unusual thing happened the next day. We were sitting around camp and down the beach walks a bull caribou. When it was almost in front of us it walked into the lake and began swimming across the bay. Two of the guys got in the zodiac and followed him at a nonthreatening distance. He swam about a quarter mile to the shore, got out and shook himself and walked into the trees. The only thing we could figure out was that he must have been bothered so much by flies that he wanted the relief of a swim. The guys however, told

Dead Caribou Bags Hunter

Frank he probably smelled him and had to get out of there by suggesting a swim would be in order for Frank also.

This was a very successful and memorial hunt. There was lots of excitement and unexpected things that happened. What might happen on our next Alaskan hunt?

Figure 41 Scott, Frank, Mike and Clint all packed.

Keith Evans

WEEKEND CARIBOU
SEPT. 15, 1995

Could I take a friend from the Lower Yukon School District village of Russian Mission, caribou hunting over the weekend and have him home for work Monday, with a caribou? I thought so, since my son and friends from Hawaii had been very successful while hunting around a remote lake, not far from where I lived in Dillingham, Alaska.

Dan Gillen was the principal at Russian Mission School. I worked with Dan for the four years I was superintendent of the Lower Yukon School District. He liked to hunt and had not had the opportunity to hunt caribou in all the time he had been in Alaska. So let's do it!

Dan arrived in Dillingham during the early evening on September 15 and we headed out to the lake immediately. Within an hour after being dropped off at the lake, we had our camp set up and the inflatable boat ready with motor attached.

The next morning we were up just as it was getting light. After a quick breakfast of oatmeal and goodies we were in the boat headed down the lake to an area where we had gotten caribou several weeks earlier. It was important for us to get Dan's caribou today because we had a mid morning pickup the next day in order for Dan to make his connections back to Russian Mission. I therefore wanted to hunt the area where we had seen the most caribou on previous hunts.

We beached the boat and headed up a game trail that ran up and over several hills. On the other side we would use our binoculars to look up a drainage area and the open tundra. Once over the hills, which took us about 45 minutes of slow walking, we stopped and took off our packs. Looking through our binoculars we spotted ten caribou walking across the drainage, heading away from us. They were too far away to shoot and moving too fast for us to cut them off. We watched them disappear over a ridge about half mile away. We were encouraged seeing caribou moving after just sitting down for about ten minutes. We saw several more caribou moving across the side of some steep hills too far away to even think about packing the meat out. After spending about 30 minutes more glassing from that spot,

Dead Caribou Bags Hunter

we moved across the drainage, over a small hill and into a lightly wooded area. We walked through some high grass and started up a small hill around some alder bushes. Out of the corner of my eye I saw something moving up on the ridge next to a row of alders. We stopped and knelt down to look under some limbs on a tree between us and whatever was moving. The first thing I thought of was a grizzly feeding on a gut pile from one of the caribou we got a couple weeks earlier.

The grass moved and rising above the grass were antlers in velvet. I motioned to Dan by raising my rifle and pointing it in the direction of the antlers. He nodded his head and got ready to shoot. The grass thinned in the direction the bull was walking and got shorter also. I hoped the bull would not turn and walk directly away from us because we would not be able to see his body and get a shot. He stopped, but we could only see his antlers. He turned his head, looking in our directions. I thought he might smell us or have sensed us being there. He then turned his head in the other direction, shook his head and took a step forward. The bull was not over 50 yards away as he stepped into an open area climbing up a small knoll, which exposed his entire body, broadside. Dan was ready. Off snapped his safety and bang. The bull dropped in his tracks. Dan was elated. His first caribou and a nice one in velvet.

Figure 42 Dan's trophy weekend bull caribou.

We dressed him out and I boned the meat so we would have less weight to carry back to the boat. We filled out packs, and sat down to get them on, with one assisting the other to stand. I was standing and helped Dan up and he took one step and yelled, "ooooooh." He immediately yelled for me to help him, as his back gave out. I grabbed his pack and eased him down to the ground. We unloaded most of his meat into my pack and he rested for a few minutes, moving his back in different directions carefully. He decided he would be able to carry a light load. I could not stand up by myself with the extra meat and I was concerned about him hurting his back again by helping me up. He insisted he could do that with out harming his back. What went through my mind at that moment was a question: did I do anything in those four previous years to Dan that he didn't like that he was now going to make me pay for it? No, Dan was not that kind of guy, but I smiled to myself about the thought. As we got started toward the boat, Dan said it was enough of a load just to be carrying his daypack and rifle.

About 45 minutes later I was resting beside the boat, not wanting to even think about going back for the rest of the meat, even though it would be half the load I just deposited in the boat. It had to be done, so after a short rest and before I started to stiffen up, I headed back over the hills and tundra for the last haul. I really didn't like the extra burden of the antlers on top of my pack. They cause one to swear if you have to go through much brush. About a half hour later I was back at the boat, bushed.

We headed back to camp late Saturday afternoon feeling good, tired, sore and hungry. We put the meat in cotton bags and hung them in the shade. Dan had a hard time moving without hurting. It even hurt to lift his fork to eat the tenderloins I cooked for dinner. Damn, hunting can be tough.

The loons put us to sleep that early evening and we woke to see an eagle perched atop a tree near our tent. We were packed and ready when the plane splashed down about ten that morning. It was a great weekend, in spite of Dan's hurt back.

Dead Caribou Bags Hunter

SUCCESS BREEDS SUCCESS
THE RETURN OF THE HAWAII GANG, PLUS
AUGUST-SEPTEMBER 1995

When people have fun and get what they want, they generally tell their relatives and friends about it. In addition, they generally want to repeat their fun and successful experiences.

Long time friend, Clint Ball, from Colorado, son Scott, Frank, Mike, and Pat from Hawaii, all had successfully hunted Alaska last year and fall into the above description. They all wanted more of the same in the fall of 1995 and they decided to bring along three more hunters. Edson, P.J. and Lincoln, Frank's brother, rounded out the camp.

I reserved the planes and got all the equipment I owned, plus some I barrowed, ready. Freshwater Adventures had a goose that would haul most of the guys and gear. We would be heading back to the remote lake where we have had good success in the past.

Since Clint was arriving before the Hawaii bunch and I only had weekends to put up with them, I charted a plane owned by Tom Johnson to haul us to the lake a couple days before the gang arrived. We got my 10' x 12' wall tent set up for cooking and my sleeping quarters and Clint's dome tent set for he and Scott. We put up tarps over them to give us more dry space. We got the zodiac pumped up, the 30 hp on it and took it for a quick spin skipping across the lake's surface.

We decided to go hiking from the camp the morning after we arrived. Heading northeast along the lake and then along a ridge away from the lake, we came upon a game trail heading east. It took us down into drainage through some woods and then up a short, but steep hillside onto open tundra. There were several small ponds on both sides of the ridge. Ducks exploded off the water as they saw us appear at the top of the hill. We sat down to glass the open tundra and a drainage that ran east west. I spotted two bull caribou feeding about four hundred yards away. We decided to go after them. We dropped down off the ridge into the drainage and walked along the base of the ridge. We had gone only about two hundred yards and decided to climb the ridge and see where the caribou were at that time. As we neared the top of the ridge we got down on our hands and knees and slowly peeked over. The two bulls had turned and were moving down off the ridge into a small drainage running perpendicular to the drainage we were following. We decided to split up. Clint would go back down into the drainage we had been following and continue up it until he had passed the drainage the bulls had taken and then cross over to the ridge running parallel to the bulls. I would go back to where we had first spotted the bulls and angle toward the bulls from the other side.

    I hurried back to where we first saw them and pulled up my binoculars, looking across the tundra up the hilly area near the drainage the bulls had taken. There, about a quarter mile away, on the side of the largest hill, was a grizzly bear. He was feeding on blueberries and was of the most unusual colors. He had four black legs from the shoulders down and the upper part of his body was a light tan. Since he was in the direction I was headed, I thought I would get a closer look a bit later. I didn't spot the caribou, so I hustled over the first two hills on the side away from the drainage the bulls were following. When I crept to the top, I looked down the drainage, but couldn't find the bulls. Where had they gone so fast? I glassed the hill where I had last seen the bear. He had moved about a hundred yards or so and was still feeding near a stand of alder bushes. As I took the binoculars away from my eyes, two bull caribou immerged out of a depression on the ridge I was following. They were about two hundred yards away. I shouldered my 375 mag., putting the cross hairs on the biggest bulls shoulder and squeezed the trigger. He dropped in his tracks. The other bull disappeared over the hill. I then looked beyond the bull to where the bear was several hundred yards away up the hill. He was looking directly at me. I started walking towards my bull and the bear turned and disappeared into the alders.

    I had the caribou partially dressed when Clint arrived. Clint saw the bulls leave the drainage heading up the ridge in front of me, but they were too far for him to shoot. Since he had not seen me, he was surprised when I shot. He was worried that the bulls would be over the ridge before I could see them. They almost made it.

Dead Caribou Bags Hunter

Figure 43 Me and my shedding bull caribou.

We boned out the meat and filled our packs. Now for the mile or so pack back to camp. We were not going to be "skunked" and we would have some good camp meat. That was testified to, as we had some nice tenderloins cooking when Scott arrived with Tom Johnson and one of the Hawaii guys.

When the goose arrived with the remaining crew and the equipment, tents and gear were all taken care of, the boat was inflated, and plans were made for the mornings hunt. It was decided that three groups would hunt together. One group would take the boat and head down the lake and the other two would hike out of camp in different directions.

The next morning was foggy, with light rain. Not an ideal hunting day, especially since you were not able to see far even with binoculars. However, everyone was anxious to hunt so little mind was given the weather.

Scott, Clint and I took the boat and headed down the lake. The others hiked out of camp, just as it was getting light enough to see. I could only hunt today and would have to leave this evening with Tom coming to pick me up and hopefully take back some meat.

Scott was hunting with his bow so we were planning on getting much close to game than before. We therefore were much more concerned about hunting in and around enough cover to hide us. After beaching the boat we headed through some alders near the shore. Just on the other side of the alders was what we were looking for, a game trail. It is so much easier walking on a packed surface rather than on the tundra, so we seek the trails. Clint would head up the trail to the southeast and we would go up to the southwest. The idea was to circle the hills and meet at the far end of the drainage.

Scott and I had not gone over a quarter mile when we spotted a nice bull caribou walking along the base of the hills running parallel to the drainage. We decided to get ahead of him and cut him off. We circled and climbed as fast as we could coming out on a flat top with open tundra. To our right, headed up the incline toward the drainage, was a young cow caribou, walking in the same direction as us. She would stop and look at us and then take a few more steps and watch us again. I was videoing her and we were both kneeling. As she neared the top of the incline, we looked to her left and could see antlers getting higher and higher. The bull had moved faster than we thought and caught us on the open tundra. When he met almost nose to nose with the young cow, he turned and walked directly towards us. The cow disappeared over the ridge. The bull was about seventy-five yards away and very curious as to what we were sitting on the tundra. I decided to see how curious he might be. I made a squeaking sound with my mouth. He looked at us for a moment and then walked about five steps closer. I repeated the sound and he walked closer yet. I was beginning to think, while filming him as I squeaked and he came closer, that if he comes about twenty more steps, Scott might be able to get a shot. My hopes died. He turned broadside and walked across the tundra into some trees and no shot for Scott. After that, he was wishing he had his rifle. It was exciting for a few minutes and we have the video to relive those moments.

We met Clint a while later. He had seen several bulls, but too far away to go after. We decided to sit and glass from the ridge we were on for a while. We saw a black bear on the far hill feeding on blueberries, which were very abundant. We had some too. It was time for us to head back to camp.

Edson, Pat, Mike and P.J. had more luck. They hiked away from camp over the rolling tundra with scattered trees and pockets of brush. The fog made it hard for them to see very far, but they had not gone far from camp before spotting two small groups of caribou. They had spread out, with Edson taking some video and Pat nearby him. P.J. and Mike were farther away. Mike moved over a small hill and there stood a bull caribou worth shooting. He dropped it with two shots.

Dead Caribou Bags Hunter

Meanwhile, P.J. had moved over a nearby ridge and looked to his left to see several nice bulls walking away from him. As it turned out, Edson was videoing them from a different position. Edson saw P.J. and yelled at him to shoot. Bang. Bang. P.J. shot Edson yelled for him to shoot the first bull again, as he had been hit. P.J. shot again and the bull went down. A long haul awaited the boys to get the meat and antlers back to camp.

Frank and Lincoln, while seeing caribou never got close enough for a shot. They were tired from hiking on the tundra for most of the day.

When Tom arrived that evening to take me and the meat back to Dillingham, arrangements were made with him to drop three groups of us at nearby small lakes for spike camps, when he brought me back Friday. We would spend a night or two looking for game seen near the lakes when we arrived the first day.

On Friday, Tom flew Frank, Lincoln and Clint to a small lake south of our main camp. Clint did not camp with them, but chose to take a tarp and string it between trees and sleep below it. Unfortunately, it rained much of the night and his attitude was not the best the next morning.

Pat, Mike, P.J. and Edson set up a camp at another small lake. Scott and I were camped on a hill overlooking a large pond. While our spike camp did not produce any game, it was scenic and relaxing. However, the spike camp idea did end with some success.

Clint spent an uncomfortable night, but got rewarded for it. He was up at the crack of light and put his gear onto his pack. He was wet, but what he didn't know was that he would be much wetter later that day and not from the rain falling on him.

Clint hunted through some small fingers of woods and open tundra about as quarter mile from Frank and Lincoln's camp. It had been light for about an hour when Clint heard a shot coming from the direction of their camp. He had the urge to head there, but decided to continue hunting where he might get a shot at something. Later that day Clint would learn that Frank walked to an open park near the tent and shot a bull caribou about 50 yards away, as it walked out of the woods.

Clint had just walked across a small open area to the edge of some woods, when he saw a legal bull moose. Legal for non-residents

Keith Evans

meant the bull must have at least three brow tines on one side of his antlers and or be fifty inches or wider across. The bull looked at him and Clint studied him through his binoculars. The bull had the required brow tines, nice long upper beams and was over fifty inches, he thought. Clint quickly dropped his binoculars away from his eyes, raised his rifle, sighted and shot. The moose trotted forward and Clint shot again. The moose faltered, but kept on going into the trees. Clint moved out of the trees where he stood and headed in the direction the moose had gone. Clint ran up over a small hill and could see the moose entering a small pond. He was about to shoot when the moose dropped. He didn't get back up. Clint walked the couple hundred yards to the pond and looked at his predicament. How was he going to get the moose out of the water that was almost covering it? Help was needed. Clint headed to find Frank and Lincoln. He hadn't gone far when Frank appeared. Having heard Clint shooting, he came to investigate. What a welcome sight.

Figure 44 Clint cleaning his moose antlers.

With a great deal of effort the two of them worked the rest of the day getting the moose gutted, cut up and out of the water. What a task! They earned that moose the hard way.

The next morning Frank and Clint decided to hike back to the area where Frank shot his caribou, while Lincoln chose to sleep in. Probably an hour or so after they left camp Lincoln rolled over to get more comfortable, when he heard something. What was it? Sounded like something splashing in the water. Probably Frank and Clint fooling around. Oh, well, he would roll over a lift the tent flap and look in the direction the splashing seemed to be coming from. As he looked out of the tent, there stepping out of the water onto the beach was a small, but legal bull moose. Wow! He quickly dropped the fly, rolled over and grabbed his rifle, loaded it, rolled back over, lifted the fly and he was still standing looking in his direction. It was hard to hold the rifle steady, but after a deep breath, bang, bang. He had his first moose ever. How easy does it get? Of course brother Frank and Clint would be back to help him process the moose.

Figure 45 Licoln with the antlers of his easy moose.

Edson, Pat, Mike and P.J. were camped at another lake nearby. Other than seeing a cow moose, they were not successful in finding any game.

Scott and I arrived back at the main camp the evening of the first day at the spike camp, whereas the other two camps stayed a second night. It was Labor Day and Scott and I decided to take the boat

Keith Evans

across the lake from the main camp and hunt the wooded area near the outlet of the lake. He would hunt with his bow and me with my rifle. After beaching the boat we spread out about fifty yards apart and started to slowly walk through the pines, which were scattered enough for us to see between them rather well. We had still-hunted through the pines for about thirty minutes and had just gotten back together, when I looked beyond and in front of him. There lying down, about eighty yards away was a moose. He looked to be all horns and they were facing us. I quietly spoke to Scott and pointed at the moose. Scott turned and looked, then whispered it was too long a shot for his bow. Since he had traveled from Hawaii, I handed him my rifle and told him to shoot the bull. After he put the gun to his shoulder and didn't shoot, I finally said, "Shoot, shoot." I was concerned the moose would get up and in one step be behind trees. Bang! The moose had stood just before Scott shot and took one step, disappearing. It sounded like he was hit. We waited about ten minutes and decided to walk over to where he had been lying. We got there and found some hair and blood. After a few more minutes we decided to follow his trail slowly. I flanked Scott on the lakeside. After walking about 100 yards I saw the bull looking back. He was lying down and struggled to his feet, very wobbly, staggering further toward the lake. While I wanted him to keep walking in that direction, as our boat was ahead of him, I also wanted him to drop. I called softly to Scott. He walked over until he could see the bull and finished him with one shot.

Dead Caribou Bags Hunter

Figure 46 Me and Scott with the antlers of his moose.

What a magnificent animal. He had a beautiful set of antlers that spread 68 inches and as it turned out, provided us with 620 pounds of boned meat. We dressed him out where he laid and propped him open with a stick to cool. Since it was getting close to dark we decided to finish the job in the morning and hope no bear found him that night. We were fortunate, as the moose was untouched when we arrived early the next morning and by ten we had the meat and antlers back in camp. What a job.

Keith Evans

Later in the morning a plane circled the camp and then landed, taxing up to the beach in front of the camp. Out climbed a Fish and Game officer. He wanted to check all licenses and the tagged antlers. Unfortunately, two of the Hawaii boys had not cut out the dates of their kills on their license, as required. They had their antlers properly tagged, but that did not make any difference to the officer, as he wrote out tickets for them. It would cost them about $100 each after getting back to Hawaii.

The next day was again foggy with light rain. Frank decided he and Lincoln would hike west of camp. They had not gone very far along the beach of the lake when they spotted a small bull caribou on the ridge. After a short sneak, Frank shot the bull. He had his second bull, which he called, "camp meat."

Scott went with Edson, Mike and Pat up a small drainage northeast of camp. Edson videoed two small groups of bull caribou too far away to shoot and moving too fast to catch up to them. After topping a hill they observed two bulls trotting broadside across the tundra, but too far away for a shot. The caribou spotted them, stopped, looked directly at them, and trotted away. As the hunters walked near some trees and alders, Pat came upon some shed moose antlers. They were bleached from the weather and belonged to a small moose. After looking for the other half for a few minutes, they climbed to the top of the hill and to their surprise, saw two bull caribou heading along the far side of the ridge. Scott wanted to shoot one with his bow. He and Mike hunched down and walked around and up the hill trying to cut them off. Scott dropped his pack and knocked an arrow. Sneaking around the last knoll they spotted the bulls. Damn! The bulls had turned down into the drainage out of range and into the alders. As they hunted further they saw several small groups of caribou.

Pat and Edson decided to cut across the drainage and see if they could get around a nice bull caribou that was feeding on the far side of the ridge. Edson was going to get the shot, so he was sneaking ahead of Pat, as they slowly worked up the ridge. Antlers appeared directly in front of them on the crest of the hill. The bull was feeding directly towards them. Edson kneeled and put down his tripod that attached to his rifle. Pat was behind him with the video camera running. As the bull fed closer his back appeared above the ground.

Dead Caribou Bags Hunter

Now the bull's entire upper body was visible. He fed closer, then raised his head and looked directly at them. He was only about thirty yards away. Pat whispered, "take him, take him, if you don't I will.' The bull took one step forward, turning his head to the side, along with the front part of his body. Bang, the horns dropped out of sight as the bull fell. He had a nice bull with antlers in the velvet.

Later that afternoon Pat, with the visibility still low, while standing among some trees, watched a single bull feeding toward him. Pat wanted his first bull and as it got into range he put his cross hairs on its shoulder just as he turned broadside. As soon as Pat shot, Edson yelled, "you got him," but Pat did not see him fall because of the fog. As Pat and Edson got to the bull, Scott approached and asked Pat to use his rifle, as he had seen a large bull too far away for his bow. Pat gave him his rifle and told Scott how far it was sighted in for. Scott left on the run in time to shoot the bull over the first hill, standing about 200 yards away.

Figure 47 Scott and his shedding bull.

As they were packing out the meat they spotted a nice grizzly feeding on one of the gut piles of a caribou gotten several days earlier.

They all got their workout hauling back meat and antlers. Scott cooled off with a bath in the lake and turned out to be camera shy.

The next day, the last of a weeks hunt, turned out to be overcast, as had each day before. The guys headed out optimistic they would see game. Pat, Mike and Edson walked out of some trees onto the edge of the tundra and spotted two bulls feeding on the side hill. Pat and Mike went around and up through a depression, coming out on the side hill behind the bulls. The bulls spotted them and started trotting. Bang, bang, they both shot. Edson was yelling, "shoot again, shoot again." Five more shots range out. One bull still walking along heard Edson yell, "finish him." Bang. Down went the bull. Pat and Mike had their second caribou each.

Scott, P.J. and Edson went out later that foggy afternoon into a wooded area. There was lots of cover for both the game and the hunters. They were moving slowly when about 50 yards away among the trees, there appeared a bull moose starring at them. Edson got his video going and the other guys checked him out with binoculars. The moose moved forward behind some more trees, yet visible between branches. After playing hide and seek for a few minutes, they decided he was too small to shoot. Just as well, as there was plenty to haul out already.

This was a most successful hunt. Four moose, Scott's being the largest, and fourteen caribou were taken. A number with nice antlers, which would help the hunters remember this hunt for many years to come.

Figure 48 Clint, Mike, Pat, Frank and me.

Dead Caribou Bags Hunter

LET'S DO IT AGAIN!
ANOTHER WEEKEND CARIBOU HUNT
SEPT. 22-24, 1995

    Walt Bromenschenkle, fellow school superintendent from the Kenai School District in Alaska, agreed to come out to hunt with me for the weekend. I had convinced him we could fly to a remote lake outside of Dillingham and find a couple of caribou over the weekend. He would arrive Friday, September 22, and we would fly out that evening.

    I had tent, inflatable boat, motor, gas, provisions and other necessary gear for the trip waiting at Freshwater Adventures, located at Dillingham Airport. It was packed in the widgeon waiting for us to board when Walt arrived.

    We had a 45-minute flight to the lake during a beautiful fall evening. As we approached the lake we noticed a hunting camp on the same side of the lake where we planned to set up our camp. That was no problem however, as there was lots of room and we had a boat to take us anywhere around the lake to hunt. We didn't notice any boat in front of their camp so we figured they would be hiking to hunt the area nearest their camp.

    We landed down the lakeshore about a quarter mile from them, unloaded our gear, and got to work putting up the tents. We sat up my 10 x 12 for cooking and a dome tent for sleeping. I always stretch a tarp over the tents to give us more dry space to sit and get into the tents if it rains. We had to find several poles and sticks to accommodate that job. As we worked we noticed we had a visitor. A seagull landed on the beach about 20 yards from us and started walking towards us peeping. It apparently had learned how to successfully beg from other campers. He managed to get us to toss him some crackers and reinforce his bad habit. He stuck around the entire two days we were there asking for handouts.

    The evening was very pleasant with the loons calling and the other ducks swimming near our camp. However, we were awakened the next morning by two owls near our camp that insisted on screeching loudly. They also decided to be our new alarm clock the next morning.

Keith Evans

After a quick breakfast we put our packs, rifles and some provisions into the boat and headed down the lake, as it was just getting light out. Ten minutes later we were at the far end of the lake and there staring at us were too steep hills to climb. I had been up them before and knew that there were game trails to follow, which made the climb on the tundra much easier. We made the game trail with little trouble and climbed steadily to the top of the hill. Once there we looked up the drainage for a mile or so with our binoculars. Nothing. We decided to sit for a while and look over the open tundra and the cover in the drainage. After fifteen minutes of seeing no game animals we decided to walk toward a ridge running parallel to the drainage. At the end of the ridge was a hill with some rock out croppings. We climbed to the top of the lower end of the ridge and stopped to glass some more. I looked up the hill near the top of the rock out-croppings and saw something black. I watched it move slowly as it stepped out of a depression and turned broadside. It was a black bear. Since they were in season, we were interested in seeing how big he was, so we moved toward him. He was feeding on blueberries and not paying any attention to us, as we were still a quarter mile away. As we walked along the ridge on open tundra, we noticed a game trail going around the side of the hill where the bear was feeding. We followed it. The walking was much easier, but it was a longer route getting to the bear. As we got to within a couple hundred yards of where we had last seen the bear, we left the game trail and snuck up over a knoll. Stopping there we sat down and glassed the area where we had last seen the bear feeding. He was gone. We got up and walked higher around some alder bushes. There, about 100 yards above us, feeding on blueberries out in the open, was the black bear. I asked Walt if he wanted to shoot him, as I shared that I thought he was just a young one and too small. After studying him through our binoculars for a few more minutes we decided he should keep eating blueberries and we slipped back around the alders and headed down the hill.

We headed up the drainage and after climbing to the top of the next small hill; we stopped to glass the area. There, in the distance, we could see five caribou feeding parallel to the lake. We had some brush cover to sneak behind to get close enough for a shot. I wanted Walt to take the first nice bull we got within range, so I suggested he follow a small drainage area to cut them off and I would circle behind them. We parted.

I had walked for about 15 minutes and had just topped a small hill, looking through some alders in the direction where I had last seen the bulls, when I heard Walt shoot once. I headed in his direction. As I walked up the drainage I noticed Walt sitting on a knoll and he appeared to be wiping his face on the right side. When I got closer I could see that he had some blood on his face. On Walt's face was a hurt-embarrassed look.

"What happened to you," I asked?

Walt explained that he saw the five bulls coming down the game trail about 200 yards away and were moving in the direction so as not to be any closer. He put down his pack, resting his rifle on it and shot. Unfortunately, he did not have the butt of the gun tight against his shoulder and the kick when he shot, caused the scope to hit him on the eyebrow, cutting it open. He drew blood, but it was his not the caribou's. The hurt part really was, he did not hit the bull he shot at.

We got the bleeding stopped and the blood cleaned off his face. He was ready to go after the bulls again. We decided to head in the general direction the bulls had gone, not expecting to see them again. We walked along the game trail the bulls were following until we came to a small drainage area. We turned and headed up it. As we rounded a small hill I saw a bull caribou alone walking in the same direction as us, but on a different game trail. He was less than 100 yards from us. I motioned to Walt to look where I pointed.

Figure 49 Walt and his bull.

He saw the bull and I said, "Take him."

Walt raised his rifle. I heard the safety click and he shot. The bull ran and stumbled. Walt shot him again and the bull dropped. He had a nice bull in spite of a cut eye.

We took some video and then dressed him out. I boned out the meat, putting three fourths of it in my pack. Walt took the antlers and the rest of the meat. We had a mile hike back to the boat. Walt had not done much packing and he was hurting by the time we got to the boat. After a short ride back to camp and taking care of the meat, we had a relaxing evening in camp.

Figure 50 Walt putting his antlers in the zodiac.

The next morning Walt was really hurting. He had a sore eye, sore legs and a strained groin. He decided not to go hunting with me down the lake in the same area we had hunted yesterday. He said he might hunt around the tent. I jumped into the boat and headed down the lake. As I neared the shore, about ready to beach the boat, I looked up and spotted a bull caribou sky lined on the ridge, walking over the top. I quickly shut off the engine as the boat glided to shore. I grabbed my rifle and pack and headed up the hill in the direction where the bull had disappeared. When I reached the top of the hill I put my binoculars to my eyes, looking for the bull. Out from behind a small clump of trees walked the bull about 500 yards away, in the valley below. He was walking away from me. I knew I could not walk fast enough to catch up to him and I needed to shoot now or forget him. I decided to count on my 375 mag. I sat down and put the cross hairs slightly above his shoulders and fired. He stopped. I shot again. He took several steps and turned in a circle. I shot again and he dropped. I took the daypack off my pack frame, as there was no use in carrying any extra weight down and up the steep hill below me.

I headed down to the bull, without my rifle, somewhat reluctantly. As I neared the bull I could see he was of medium size and would certainly require two trips to haul out the boned meat. It was about ten when I shot him and by two I had the last load to the boat. What a workout hauling about 140 pounds of meat up and down some steep, brush spotted hills. I was bushed. When I dumped my pack and meat into the boat on the last trip I noticed that the brace running across the middle of the pack frame was busted. I wondered why my shoulders started feeling more strain as I headed up the hill.

I got back to camp by 2:30 p.m. to find Walt just coming down the beach towards the camp. He had taken a short walk near camp, but didn't see anything. He was feeling a little better having taken the walk.

We had two bulls and I teased him that mine had wider antlers than his. However, that was because I had cut the skull plate down the middle so I could pack the horns easier, so now I could stretch them to flat out if I wanted.

Figure 51 Me and the "giant" antlers in camp.

Keith Evans

The weather had been great for the entire time and especially this morning, with calm winds, warm temperatures and sunny skies. What fond memories of a successful weekend caribou hunt in Alaska.

RETIRED, TIME TO HUNT
AUGUST 1997

A long time friend of mine, Bob Mills, contacted me about taking him and his two sons caribou hunting in Alaska. I had just retired from Alaska after spending nine years as a school administrator there. I own, with a partner, about 80 acres on a remote lake, where we built a cabin. I planned on being at the cabin in late August and early September, so I agreed to take Bob and son's caribou hunting. He and son Joe would travel from Michigan and son Mike would travel from Anchorage.

Since son Scott, Clint Ball and Mike Rosa had planned on hunting with me for a couple weeks, we would just have seven hunters in camp for the first week, instead of four.

I decided to be at the cabin a couple days before anyone else arrived to get things organized and gear pulled together for the flight out to the remote lake where we would hunt. I left for the lake the late evening of August 29, arriving about an hour before dark. This was the same lake we had hunted from four previous years, with great success. We had taken both caribou and moose from the area and felt certain we would again have opportunities at getting caribou, which everyone would be hunting.

When the charter pilot taxied up to the beach where we had camped on previous hunts, there had been a change since last year. The campsite was on a small peninsula, with a stream entering the lake on the east side of it. Beavers had made dams farther up the stream years earlier. What I found on the beach was a large pile of sticks constituting a beaver's lodge. I had never seen one entirely on dry land before. It was near the spot where I had erected my 10' x 12' wall tent last year. There was still plenty of room for my tent, but I was to learn that the beaver that owned the lodge didn't appreciate my uninvited presence.

Once I got my tents, cooking gear, inflatable boat, motor, gas, etc out of the plane, I set to work erecting the big wall tent. I had never put it up alone. It had a metal interior frame, which I laid out on the ground. I then spread the tent over the frame and crawled under the tent. I started putting the frame together and that caused me to swear a number of times. It was difficult trying to see what color matched in the dim light and then to try and hold the frame in place and stretch the tent over it. I wondered why I had not had a test run some time earlier. I finished the job just before it was real dark. The dome tent went up in just a few minutes and the large tarp I put over the tents to give us more dry space, was the last chore before opening my cot and sleeping bag.

As I stretched out ready for a good nights sleep, something unexpected happened. Bang. Bang. I didn't know it, but my neighbor was upset with me. Bang. Bang. He was mad and was making a point of it. I slipped out of my sleeping bag and opened the tent flap and there, twenty feet away was the cause of the noise. A large beaver was swimming back and forth along the beach near the lodge, slapping his tail on the water. Talking to him did no good. I decided that I might as well go back to my bag and hope he would get tired of being unfriendly.

I think I drifted off to sleep for a few minutes after trying to compose a song called, "beaver, beaver, bang, bang." The next thing I realized I was startled by a more disturbing sound. The walls of the 10' x 12' tent were flapping furiously. I thought the tent was going to take off. I grabbed my flashlight, turned it on and wondered if a grizzly was trying to turn the tent over or was just knocking hard to get in. No, it was just a very strong wind blowing. I moved the coleman lantern that was hanging directly above me, just in case it got tired of hanging there. I listened and concluded that the wind and resultant waves had caused Mr. Beaver to stop banging his tail, which I would have gladly traded for no wind.

As I felt the tent shuddering, I also heard the tarp flapping furiously. It was just a few minutes and there was a ripping sound and even more flapping. I grabbed the flashlight, pulled on pants, shirt and boots, then headed outside to check the damage. Two eyelets were torn loose from the edge of the tarp. Now what was I going to do? Well, improvise of course. I found two small stones and placed them near the spots where the eyelets gave out. I covered the stones with part of the tarp, and then tied the rope around the stone. Back to bed I went, hoping to get a little sleep before dawn.

Dead Caribou Bags Hunter

Scott, Clint and Mike would be arriving sometime in the late afternoon. I needed to inflate my boat and test the motor, as it had not been run since last fall.

Everything was ready when they arrived. I had decided I was going hunting northwest of the camp because I had seen some caribou feeding in that area when I was checking out the motor.

The next morning after they arrived we headed toward the area where I had seen the caribou. We walked along the beach and then up a ridge, through a drainage covered by woods, and up a hill to the open tundra. We stood and glassed the open area. We spotted two bulls feeding on a ridge on the other side of the drainage to the east of us. We decided to split up. Clint and Mike would cut across the drainage behind the bulls and try to get on the far side of them. Scott would try to sneak on them from behind and I would try to get in front of them by following the ridge we were on and then cut across the drainage.

About twenty minutes later I was sneaking over a little hill, after crossing the drainage and to my left about 200 yards away, were the bulls. They had moved faster than we had anticipated. I didn't have time to do much thinking, as they were getting farther away with each step. I decided to trust my 375 magnum, putting the crosshairs on the shoulder of the largest one and squeezed the trigger. He dropped in his tracks. We would certainly have camp meat. It was great to be the old man and have three young bucks to haul the meat back to camp.

Figure 52 Me and my bull.

It was August 31 and today a widgeon would fly in bringing the Mills boys. Fortunately, the weather had improved considerably. There was little wind and lots of sunshine. It was pleasant setting up their tents and enjoying an evening's meal of sweet and sour caribou.

The next morning I took the three Mills boys and headed to the east end of the lake in my boat, just as it was getting light out. Scott, Clint and Mike were going to hunt to the north of camp where they had lots of luck in the past.

We beached the boat and hit a game trail heading through a small stand of alders, up the first of several hills. Once we topped the last hill, about 15 minutes later, immediately in front of us to the east, stood a bull caribou. He was looking directly at us. I looked at him through my binoculars and decided he was too small. We could take a chance on doing better, since this was the first day.

I heard Joe say, " He is a nice one."

That was what I thought when I saw my first bull caribou. After hunting whitetail deer, seeing caribou antlers for the first time, even the small ones look big.

I told Joe to hold his rifle in both hands and wave it back and forth over his head. He looked at me kind of funny, but did it anyway. The bull was about 100 yards away and as Joe waved his rifle over his head, the bull walked towards us for about twenty steps. He stopped and looked at us some more and then turned to the north and walked up a ridge. I had my video going all the time. He stopped sky lined and looked at us. He then performed a move, which I have seen caribou do when they are spooked. He raised both front feet off the ground in a little hop and trotted away.

We then started walking around the ridge, looking towards the lake and the valley directly below us. After getting around to the south side we spotted two bulls walking towards the lake, directly away from us. We spotted a game trail and started trotting down it in the direction of the bulls. There were some bushes and a few trees ahead of us, which gave us some cover. Joe was behind me and he said he wanted the biggest bull. I got him up next to me as we rounded some bushes. The bulls were about 150 yards away, quartering away from us. Joe took aim and fired. The bull shrugged, but moved towards the lake. We followed and after going through some brush and over some small knolls, we came upon the bull, still

Dead Caribou Bags Hunter

alive. Joe shot him once more. We only had a couple of blocks to get him to the boat. Nice work, Joe.

Figure 53   Mike, Joe and me with Joe's bull.

Figure 54   Me and Joe with bull in boat.

We then climbed back to the south ridge top where we had seen the bulls. Getting out our binoculars, we glassed the area and to the south were three more bulls walking to the west, paralleling the lake. We whistled to see if they would stop. One bull stopped and looked around for just a moment, then continued with the other two over the ridge. We took off trotting towards the rim of the ridge. When we got there a couple minutes later, we spotted the three bulls at the base of the hill. They were just starting up a small hill. Bob sat down, thumbed off his safety and fired once, twice, three times, and four times. Mike fired once, twice, three times and four times. The biggest bull, which they were shooting at, seemed confused as to which way to run. He went one way a few steps and then back another way. While Mike was shooting Bob was reloading and when Mike stopped shooting Bob fired two more shots. The bull fell down. I wondered if it was from fright or if he was hit.

We headed down to the bull and after checking him out, decided that he had been hit just once. The other nine shots just kept him confused.

Figure 55 Bob, Joe and Mike with Bob's bull.

We had a nice view of the lake from the hill, which we were on and it would be downhill for packing the meat. However, walking across the tundra, even downhill, is work when packing out meat. The lake was about three quarters of a mile away and with four of us packing; each load was not too heavy. Maybe 35 pounds each, or there abouts. After getting there we decided to head back to camp and spend the remainder of the day there.

Scott, Mike and Clint had not seen a bull big enough to shoot. They were disappointed and spoiled from seeing bulls quite easily on previous hunts in that area. They did see a sow grizzly bear with two cubs.

It was a beautiful evening. The weather was being good to us and we tried to compliment it with alder grilled silver salmon, which I brought, and caribou tenderloin steaks.

Figure 56 Mike and Scott with Mike's bull.

The next morning Clint, Scott and Mike got overly ambitious and walked a mile or so from the east end of the lake to some ponds. They saw some bull caribou in that direction and split up sneaking on them. Mike was able to get close enough to shoot, so he put a medium size bull down with one shot. Of course he caught hell from his two packers, because of the long haul back to the lake.

Figure 57 Mike and Clint with Mike's bull.

I took the Mills boys on a long hike along the south side of the lake where I had seen some caribou. After hiking the morning we topped onto a plateau where we ate lunch and the Mills boys laid down for a nap. It was warm and it turned out to be a day of exercise and enjoyment of the out of doors.

Figure 58 Joe and Mike joined dad Bob for a nap.

Dead Caribou Bags Hunter

Mike Mills had not gotten a caribou, but he did get some shooting at the bull Bob shot. Scott and Clint had not found a bull either. I took the Mills boys to the east end of the lake where we were successful the first day. After climbing the ridge where we saw Bob's bull, we split up to walk over some small hills. Mike and Joe were together and Bob and I were together. Shortly after we split, we heard shooting. Mike had seen a bull go over a ridge, near the same area where Bob shot his bull. Mike saw the bull at the base of the hill and shot three times. He thought the bull was hit, but shot a fourth time knocking the bull down. When he got up to the bull it was still alive, so he finished it with another shot.

Figure 59 Joe and Mike with Mike's bull.

While we were dressing out the bull, I looked to the west, on the south side of the lake, and saw three bulls feeding on the open tundra.

We decided to head back to camp with Mike's bull and once there the Mills boys decided to stay in camp. I decided to jump back in the boat and head to the south side of the lake to see if the bulls I saw were still around. I beached the boat on the south shore and walked behind a stand of alders for several hundred yards. I then walked across some open tundra, to some more alders, between me and where I thought the bulls might be feeding. Once I got to the alders, I crawled through them and came out behind some bushes. From over the tops of the bushes I could make out a single bull feeding about 200 yards away. His antlers where partly in velvet on one side and ragged on the other.

I decided to take him. The 375 spoke and it did the job again. The bull dropped in his tracks with one shot. I decided after dressing him out that some help would be in order. The Mills boys had heard the shot and were waiting for the news. With their help, it made a one man's hard job, easy.

Figure 60 Me and my bull.

Scott, Mike and Clint decided to hunt near the lake outlet where Scott and I got his 68" antlered moose a couple years earlier. They had just come out of woods near some ponds and started walking along the shore of the lake, when a bull caribou jumped up. Scott was in front and I don't know who was most surprised, the bull or Scott. Well, Scott recovered the quickest, that's for sure, as he pulled out his 44-magnum pistol and shot the bull. He managed to do that with a cast on his shooting hand. He had been in a car-bike accident in Kauai. A young guy passed him on a double yellow line as Scott made a left hand turn. He smacked the windshield and ended up on the side of the road, lucky to be alive.

Dead Caribou Bags Hunter

Figure 61 Scott and his pistol shot bull.

That caribou was the last one shot on this trip. We ended up with six caribou. Clint was the only one who didn't get one. That was unusual, as he has had good luck on all previous hunts, getting both caribou and a moose.

Figure 62 Me, Mike- kneeling, Clint, Bob, Joe, and Mike- kneeling.

Keith Evans

On September 6, a goose from Fresh Water Adventures picked us up and dropped us off at my cabin, with the exception of Mike Mills, who went on to Dillingham with them. Mike flew back to Anchorage that night. I took Joe and Bob to Dillingham the next day to get them on their way back to Michigan.

Scott, Clint and Mike were staying with me at the cabin for another week of hunting. Unfortunately, it ended in tragedy. Read: Dead Caribou's Revenge.

BUSH PILOT BLUNDERS
1998

I decided to head up to the cabin early enough to get some work done and to do a little fishing before going hunting. I arrived at Dillingham, Alaska August 27 and was met at the airport by friends, Dave and Tawnja Powers. I stayed with them overnight the 27th and 28th. My boat and trailer, along with my pickup were stored at Dave and Tawnja's house. When I started my pickup to leave for the cabin on the morning of the 29th, it would only run on two cylinders. Dave was gracious as usual and let me use his truck.

I drove the 25 miles to Lake Aleknagik, launched my boat and was at the cabin in 30 minutes. When I had finished putting all my gear and food in the cabin, I decided to fire up the weed whacker and cut some of the long grass around the cabin. You have to do those kinds of things when the weather is right and you are not ready to put a rifle or fishing pole in your hand. For the next five days I worked around the cabin. I stained the outside cabin trim, put a metal roof on the outhouse, varnished the front of the steam house and my boat seat, and hauled stone from the beach to refurbish our path from the beach to the cabin and outhouse.

On Sept. 4, I launched the boat and headed back to the landing and Dave's truck. I had to go to Dillingham to pick up son Scott, brothers, Mike and Pat Rosa from Kauai, Hawaii. All three were coming to hunt and fish. They all had been here to hunt and fish before. I picked them up from the airport and we had to go downtown to pick up a few food items and Mike had to get some beer. While Mike drinks in moderation, he does like a couple of cold ones after a days hunting or fishing.

We stopped to see Tom Johnson at his floatplane base at Shannon's Pond before heading to the cabin. Tom shared with us the success that some other hunters had on a lake north of the one we intended to go to for our hunt. He said they got a bull moose that had an antler spread of 60 inches. It almost walked into their camp, so they didn't have far to pack the meat. He recommended that we go up to Rat Lake, because not only were the moose around, but there also were some caribou, which we were looking for. We told him we would think about it and would let him know.

We headed to the cabin from Tom's place and arrived without incident. We had planned on doing a lot of fishing before going hunting and I planned on getting some help from them to build a shed on the back of the cabin to house the generator and batteries.

We had fun catching silver and red salmon, dolly varden and pike.

On the evening of September 9th, Tom sat his floatplane down in front of the cabin. The weather was a little marginal, with rain, when Scott got into the plane with gear for the trip to Rat Lake. Since there was not any room for anyone else, Scott would go alone to find a place for us to camp and begin scouting the area for our arrival sometime the next day. Tom and Scott took off in heavy winds and almost got slammed into the lake. Tom could not chance another trip.

We were scheduled to leave with Tom Schlagel the next day in his beaver. Unfortunately, when Tom arrived the next morning and we loaded all our gear, we did not have room for my inflatable boat and motor, so we had to leave it at the cabin.

Rat Lake was small and shallow, located in a drainage area for the surrounding hills and a small mountain. Scott had pitched his tent on some uneven tundra, next to the shore, as there was no level ground, which made for some interesting sleeping positions at night. We put up my 10X12 wall tent, which would be used as the cookhouse and storage "shed," on the beach next to his tent. Pat and Mike erected their tent on the tundra near Scott's. After finishing our house keeping chores, we headed out to explore and look for caribou. Scott and I headed in one direction and Mike and Pat in another. It wasn't long after we parted when we heard several shots. Pat and Mike told us later that they had just left the lakeshore and had gone up through some woods when they spotted a small herd of caribou out on the open tundra. They were headed toward a wooded area several hundred yards away, but were within a 100 yards or so from them. They both shot and got a nice bull.

Scott and I went through a wooded area along the lake and then up along the top of a hill out to the open tundra. In our glassing we spotted a nice grizzly bear about a half-mile away. We watched it feed on blueberries along the top of a hill for about a half hour, before it ambled over the top of the hill heading towards woods on the other side.

Along toward the late afternoon we spotted several caribou about a mile away on the open tundra. There was a hill between them and us, which could be used to cover our sneak. We decided to split up, with Scott trying to cut in ahead of them and me heading directly at them. When you watch caribou walk they don't seem to be moving very fast. We found that they move faster at a slow walk than we do at a fast walk. I had just started up the hill I was using for cover, when I heard a shot. I walked to the top of the hill to find Scott. He had gone up a ditch and was coming out the upper end when he looked to the north of him and there stood the caribou. They had gotten past him. However, standing and looking at him was a mistake. When I saw him after the shot, he was standing looking down at a nice bull. Two hours later we had all the meat and horns back in camp.

Non-resident hunters can take two caribou, so Pat, Mike, and Scott wanted to find another one each and I wanted one for the freezer. Pat and Mike headed back to the same area where they had gotten their caribou the day before. Scott and I decided to split up. He was going to hunt where he shot his bull, also. I decided to explore the area where we had seen the grizzly feeding. We left camp together and then split going our separate ways. I was moving slowly up a tree covered slope when I saw some movement in front of me about 30 yards away. I stopped, and bending down to look under tree limbs, there on the game trail I was following stood a beautiful gray wolf. He was looking directly at me. Before I could move, he jumped across the trail and disappeared into the brush. I walked cautiously forward to the spot where he had been standing, looking in the direction he had gone. I was hoping to see him again, but no such luck. He had slipped away like a ghost.

I walked out of the woods along a ridge, which led out onto the tundra area and to the top of the hill where we had seen the grizzly feeding. It was obvious that grizzlies had frequented that area because there were lots of bear droppings. I sat on that hill glassing the large drainage area to the north and spotted a grizzly moving along a creek. He seemed to have a destination in mind, as he walked steadily until he was in the brush out of sight. I turned and then glassed to the south out across the open tundra. I had heard shots coming from the southeast earlier. Pat, Mike and Scott where east of me, so they could have been shooting and probably were, because we had not seen any other hunters in the area. I had been glassing for about a half an hour when I saw two bull caribou, somewhat separated, but heading in the same northwest direction. I watched them trot along and then I glassed ahead of the first one to see where he might be headed. I noticed two hunters seated on the tundra east of a small pond, directly in line with the caribou's route. At first I thought it was Pat and Mike, but looking closer, they were not wearing the same type of clothing that Pat and Mike had on. I concluded that they were two hunters who walked from an adjacent lake around the base of the small mountain to the northwest.

The lead caribou got to within about 50 yards of the seated hunters, when one raised his rifle and shot. The bull staggered and he shot again. The bull fell and didn't get up. The second bull turned and headed due north. It looked like he might come within shooting range of me. I had been videoing the two bulls and unfortunately my battery warning sign started flashing. However, I needed to put it down and pick up my rifle in case the bull continued toward me. On he came, unaware of me seated on top of the hill. As he trotted along the base of the hill I waited until he got about 100 yards away, then put the cross hairs on his front shoulder and squeezed the trigger. He dropped in his tracks. Now the work began. I had just about finished dressing him out when I looked up and here comes son Scott. What a welcomed sight. Now he could carry the heaviest load of meat and we would only have to make one trip. Scott had not seen any caribou, but he had seen a nice bull moose and a black bear.

We got back to camp to find some caribou meat hanging in a new spot. Pat and/or Mike, or both, must have gotten a caribou. They had gone back to get the rest of the meat and returned about a half hour later. We sat down and exchanged stories. They were lucky, as they shot their second bull each much closer to camp than their first ones.

We had a relaxing evening and went to bed early.

Tom Johnson arrived the next morning in his 180 bringing John Givens, an attorney from Anchorage, and his father James, from Texas, who I had agreed to take on a caribou hunt. That came about because Mike Mills, a fellow attorney in the same law firm, had been on a successful hunt with me last year.

Mike and Pat had filled their licenses, so they decided to ride back with Tom on his return trip and take their meat to be processed and then go to the cabin and fish until we came on the 17th. So, when the Givens had emptied the plane of their gear, Pat and Mike filled it with theirs, themselves and Scott, who also decided to go back. He was going to help them, but he would also pick up the inflatable and motor and bring it back out on the 15th. Rick Grant would be hired to haul him out in his beaver. Scott had to stay in town because of bad weather so he helped Tom by bulldozing part of a new landing strip.

Once I got John and James settled, we took off walking toward the area where Pat and Mike had shot their caribou. We saw several, but they were too far away to go after. The next day turned out to be the same, no shoot able caribou. In fact, we saw only three. However, we did see a black bear.

The following day we had hiked to the south end of the lake and were headed up a drainage on the open tundra, when I spotted a caribou within sneaking range. We slipped into a ditch that had some protective brush along the edge between the caribou and us. Before starting the sneak I told them that the caribou was a cow. She had small horns and I wondered if either of them would want to shoot her. James said he would take her, as we were not seeing many animals and the time was getting short. As we got to the end of the ditch and crawled under a bush on a knoll, James had just taken a prone position to shoot when the caribou started trotting broadside about 50 yards away. He dropped it with one shot. We dressed her out and I had a short trip back to camp with a light load of meat on my back.

Scott flew in the morning of the 15th with Rick Grant in his beaver. I asked Rick to come back and pick us up on the 17th, which he agreed to do. I asked him to check with Tom Schlagel, as he was coming out also with his beaver, because we had two beaver loads to haul back. Rick agreed to check with Tom to coordinate the pick-up time.

I inflated my boat and John and I motored to the south end of the lake. We hiked a mile or so across the tundra before seeing a small bull caribou alone. After sneaking along a line of brush we got within shooting distance and John put him down with a single shot. I was glad that bull was small because a mile pack across tundra is a lot of work, even with half of a small caribou.

Figure 63 John and James with Pat and Mike's antlers

Scott hunted along the lake and saw a nice bull moose, which he wasn't licensed to shoot. I had the moose license, but I was too busy helping the Givens get their caribous, that I didn't hunt for a moose. In fact, when John and I were motoring back to camp with his caribou, on the shore about 200 yards away and a quarter mile down the shore from camp, there stood a large bull moose. He had a spread of antlers that looked better than 60 inches wide. However, it was the day after the season was closed. To add insult to injury, as we watched that big bull, a second bull walked out of the brush. He was just a little smaller with a different configuration to his antlers. Either of these could have been the bull Scott had seen earlier.

Along about 5:00 pm on September 17, Tom Schlagel landed to pick us up, but no Rick Grant. We loaded his beaver full of gear, with John and James squeezed in between.

Tom's parting words were, "I'll be back to pick you up." I thought that was strange since Rick was suppose to have coordinated their joint pickup time, but I didn't think much about it at the time. Tom took off and Scott and I waited thinking Rick would show up and that Tom had just misspoke himself. However, no one came.

We had everything packed except the dome tent and our sleeping bags. The next day the 18th became windy and overcast. No one showed and in came the rain with gusts of wind over 50 knots. That night the wind blew so hard it broke a metal roof rod and bent the other one. This allowed the tent material to collapse on us bringing with it the rainwater. The water leaked into the tent and I was bailing it out of the low spots with a rubber boot. We were not happy campers. Morning couldn't come soon enough.

Figure 64 Me after a wet night.

Figure 65 Scott trying to look happy!

The next day we again stayed in camp thinking someone would show up, rather than go hunting and be away from it if someone came. The weather, while cloudy, was within flying minimums and wouldn't stop a plane from coming after us. While waiting today we combed the shoreline for any dead wood we could find. The fire felt good and gathering the wood gave us something to do. One good thing happened. I was sitting down looking up the shoreline, when about 300 yards away, a wolverine stepped off the bank. He had his nose to the ground as he headed our way down the beach. I decided that he would look great on my video, so I stood up to get my camera and he stopped, looked at us, then jumped onto the bank and disappeared.

The morning of the 20th came clear and cool. We were beginning to wonder if we were every going to be picked up. While we had enough food for several more days, we were now past due to be home and Scott to be back at work.

I had a hand-held radio and because there had not been any airplanes flying in our area, we could not use it to contact anyone for help. However, it was clear this morning and we expected planes to be flying. We were not disappointed. Off in the distance flying towards Dillingham, we heard, and then spotted the plane. I was able to make contact with the pilot and I requested he contact Tom Johnson and tell him we needed to be picked up. He said he would do that. We knew Tom's 180 could not carry all our gear, but we would worry about that after he arrived. Tom was a very dependable and helpful sort of guy. We felt much better believing Tom would be out to get us sometime later today.

A few hours later that morning we saw another plane heading north. As it got closer to use we could see it was a beaver and then it turned toward us and landed on our lake. He taxied to the beach. It was Rick Grant.

He shut it down and got out asking, "What are you guys still doing here?"

We said, "We are still here because you didn't come to pick us up."

He said he called Tom Schlagel about coordinating pickup time on the 17th and Tom told him he would take care of us. Rick said he didn't want to infringe on his business so he assumed Tom would take care of us. We were a bit upset having gone though three extra days waiting on the beach doing nothing, being in a blowned down wet tent for most of one night, having loved ones worrying about us because we were not home, missing work without notification of employer, and not having pilots do what they agreed to do. I told him that I specifically requested a charter with him for our return and he had agreed. Therefore, he should not have allowed Tom Schlagel to say he would take care of us. I then told him I wanted him to load up our gear and take us back to Dillingham. Scott got very pissed and unloaded on the pilot. He became somewhat mad and jumped back in his plane saying he had hunters to pick up and flew away. After Scott cooled down he told me it would have been smarter to wait until we had a ride to town before blowing his cool.

Tom Johnson flew in that evening. He said he had talked to Rick on the radio and had also been contacted by the pilot I had radioed that morning. Tom said he could shuttle, in two trips, our gear over to an island where Rick said he would haul all the gear Tom could not carry in his plane, since he only had a partial load with his hunters. Tom also mentioned that Mike Rosa had called him wondering what had happened to us since we had not returned on the 17th, as planned.

We waited on the island for just a short time before Rick landed and we loaded all the gear on the beach into his beaver. We arrived back in Dillingham about 6:00 pm on the 20th, three days later than we had planned

Scott and I stayed with Tom Johnson at his house that night after going down town to buy five steaks, salad and beverages. While there, I called a friend, John Norman, whom lives at a fishing lodge near my cabin, and whom we sold the land to so he could build it. I found out in our conversation that he had transported Mike and Pat to the launching area when they left to go home. My boat was therefore still at the cabin, so we needed a ride from the launching area to the cabin. We arranged a time to meet there and I hired a guy to drive us to the lake the morning of the 21st. John got us to the cabin before noon and we got everything put away and jumped in my boat to head back to Dillingham. We wanted to see if we could get a flight out that night. When we got to Dave Power's home we called the airport to see if there was space available to get to Anchorage. They said for us to get over there right away, as the plane was late from Anchorage and they did have space if we got there in time. Off we went. We arrived in Anchorage in the early evening and Scott made connections to be on his way at 8:00 pm that night. I got home the next night.

We ended up getting 8 caribou, even though there were not many around. We saw three bull moose, a wolf, grizzly bear, black bear and a wolverine. Plus, learning something about charter pilots. The cost of transportation to and from the lake was $3100. Hunting in Alaska can be frustrating, unpredictable and costly.

Dead Caribou Bags Hunter

SOLITUDE AND SURPRISES
ALASKA
8-18-00—9-6-00

Figure 66 Lake Aleknagik and property.

Figure 67 Hard to beat this beauty.

Keith Evans

I left Traverse City at 7:30a.m. on August 18th with mixed feelings. While I looked forward to going to the cabin and being in the "wilds", I also felt it was going to be lonely. Having someone to share your experiences with seems to make them more meaningful and enjoyable. Not having son Scott along makes the trip much different, as he has been along on many in the past eight years.

Got to Minneapolis and changed planes twice. The captain on the first plane didn't like the way the rudder operated so two hours later we were on another plane out. I therefore only had a two hour wait in Anchorage, rather than a four hour wait. We left there 45 minutes late and arrived at a packed Dillingham airport.

Dave Powers, a local doctor and friend, was there to meet me. I stayed with Dave and his wife Tawnja over night. Tawnja worked in the Dillingham City School's central office with me for the three years I served as superintendent for the district.

After a pleasant evening and a good nights sleep, I got things together by noon to head for the cabin. Before driving the 25 miles to the lake I went to town and took care of getting my hunting license. I only needed to pick up caribou tags. Since Fish and Game was not open I could not get my early moose permit. If I come early another year I need to plan on arriving on a weekday, so all the agencies would be open.

Dave said he and Tawnja were going to come up to hunt.

I therefore would not be hunting alone, at least for one day.

I left with Tawnja's vehicle and Dave's 30hp engine, which he hooked up. Dave insisted I take his engine, saying it needed to be run since it had been sitting around for so long.

I stopped and talked to Dennis Dean whom I found working on his boat and a flat tire on his trailer. Dennis said he would come up to hunt, also.

I drove the 25 miles to Lake Aleknagik and arrived there about 1:00 p.m. Wow, what a difference. There was a new cement pad for launching boats, toilets, parking lot and landscaping.

I launched my boat and got the motor started. However, it wouldn't stay running. A guy came over and asked me if he could spell me on pulling the cord. He introduced himself as Mike Moore, the new high school principal in Dillingham.

When I told him my name he said, "I have heard a lot of positive things about you." I shared that I had heard the same about him.

I got the engine to run until I was about twenty feet from the landing and then it stopped. I started it again and it ran again for another 20-30 ft, at no more than a fast idle, and stopped again. Three and one half-hours later and two bloody – blistered fingers, I arrived at the cabin. The last quarter mile or so the engine didn't want to run at all, so I paddled to the point of land going into the cabin then towed the boat along shore the rest of the way. I was fortunate that the lake was calm or I would have still been out there.

One boat full of women and kids did come towards me while I was trying to start it once more, but I got it started so I waved them off. I tried everything to make it run. I knew it was not getting gas properly, but nothing I did with the choke or throttle made any difference. About the best I could get was about a three-second spurt, at a speed just above an idle. If I were lucky, it would repeat that sequence several times, and then stop. If I weren't lucky it would stop after one sequence. Fortunately, it kept starting. My arm and chest was sore from all the action, plus my first three fingers on my left hand had broken blisters on the inside and were bleeding. It normally takes me 30 minutes to get to the cabin from the launching area.

At 10:00 a.m. Sunday the 20th I walked around half our shoreline and cut back to the cabin. I only saw one set of moose prints. I expected Dave and Tawnja to come up to hunt, but they didn't show up.

Some changes had taken place in the cabin since last year.

My partner in the cabin, Mark Vingoe, had talked his brother into helping him put down a wood floor over the plywood to replace the carpet and to put wood upstairs on the walls. It all looked good.

I took a paddle in Mark's kayak last night and it was quiet and fun. It was a calm evening, but I didn't see any game.

When you get up each morning you automatically check out the weather because you have to go outside to the bathroom. It reminded me of when I was a kid.

It was cloudy this morning, just like yesterday. Today there is a slight breeze and a temperature of about 50 degrees.

Keith Evans

When I came up to the cabin I brought the gas tank for my Tohatsu engine, just in case I needed to use it. I figured I should run it some since it has not been run for a year. Unfortunately, I had a senior moment and forgot to get the gas line. Guess I thought it would be with the engine at the cabin. I was going to put it on the boat to replace Dave's motor. Now I can't do that. I don't like the thought of a three plus hour trip back to the landing and a drive back to Dave's. Maybe I should take my neighbor, John, up on his offer to let me borrow one of his motors. However, I don't really like to do that.

I decided to take the kayak out for another paddle. John said there are two smaller bull moose around the property and three down where I got shot. Two of them are good size. I paddled around for several hours, but did not see any moose.

Teresa, Duane, son Blake and three of their friends stopped. Teresa had to pick up her guitar; they had been using the cabin. We had a nice visit. I asked Duane to call Dave and have him bring up my gas line when he comes up to his cabin. I rented an apartment from Teresa and Duane for several years while in Dillingham.

Wonders never cease to happen. Dave and Tawnja stopped Sunday night after Teresa and all left. It was about 10:00 p.m. I told them about my problem getting up to the cabin. Dave was very apologetic and got in my boat to see if he could determine what was wrong. Didn't take him but a minute to see that he had put the gas line on backwards. He changed it and the engine ran fine. I never thought to check that because he had hooked it up and I assumed he knew what he was doing. They didn't stay long and headed back to their cabin. Dave came up the next morning and we headed down to the area where I got shot. We saw a cow moose while walking in one of the open parks together and when we separated, Dave saw a grizzly bear. I took a hike around the area where I got shot in 97. When I got back down near the spot where we separated, I took my pack off and laid it on the ground and noticed that my bag was unzipped. Earlier, Dave had handed me my video camera to take some pictures of the moose and I hung it around my neck. I looked inside my bag for my 35mm camera and it was not there. I thought I must have dropped it on my walk. I retraced my steps, but didn't find it. When I got back

Dead Caribou Bags Hunter

to the spot where I started, I looked down and noticed something under a limb of a bush. There was the camera. What a relief.

I went with Dave back to his cabin and then into Dillingham to pick up our moose permit and some building things he needed for his cabin. We got back to his cabin about 2:00 and put up ceiling insulation, plus a vapor barrier. We had to stand on high ladders and walk a plank between them. It made one careful and a bit nervous. We got done about 6:30, ate and headed to my cabin. It was rough riding as the wind had picked up. Actually, it pounded the hell out of us until Dave slowed the engine down. We stopped and hunted the same area where Dave and I hunted earlier. Saw nothing.

Dave and Tawnja stayed overnight with me and Dave and I got up and went hunting to the spot where he had seen a bull while flying his plane. It was northwest of the cabin beyond the lodge on the right hand side. I saw a moose going through the brush. I could not determine if it was a bull, because of the thick brush.

Dave and Tawnja left about 1:00 after we got some stones out of the jet unit. We had picked them up while motoring through some shallow water. The stones prevented the engine from going fast enough to get on step.

After they left I decided to go down the lake fishing and caught a dolly varden about 3#s. There was no one else around and the fishing was very pleasant. I had half of the dolly for dinner.

I have not been able to get the hot water heater to work. Taking a bath in a pan isn't much fun. It was 35 this morning.

It is 9:00 p.m. and the sun is still high in the sky. It is a beautiful night, but lonely, quiet and peaceful. Just got cleaned up and am heading for bed.

Got up at 7 and had my breakfast of oatmeal, glass of milk, hot chocolate, wheat bread, peanut butter and jam. Got in the kayak and paddled around to the north bay and walked through the woods into the open fields northeast of our property. Didn't see anything. Came back, stained trim on the cabin as high as I could reach standing on planks resting on two sawhorses, with a chair on top of the planks. Couldn't find any ladders. Thought maybe Mark had loaned them to John, but I didn't feel like going over there to see.

I mixed some more gas and straightened up the steam house. It started to rain so I will repack the boxes I took apart to get bedding for Dave and Tawnja and do some reading. If I'm lucky, a moose will revisit the trees rubbed in front of the cabin.

I took out the bathroom sink to replace the faucet that Mark could not get to stop leaking. It needed to be done because it leaked the whole 35 gallons out of the tank over night. Works fine now.

I just got it done when Tom Johnson flew in with two fellows working for BIA. They were inspecting native allotments that were being sold for any significant historical remains. The law requires such inspections. They stayed about one hour and didn't seem in any rush to leave, probably because it was raining outside. Tom said he would stop back before I left to give me a sight seeing ride.

I went to bed about 7:30 and was awakened from my thoughts at 8:00 by a knock on the door. I had not heard anyone motor in, but when I looked out the window I saw two boats and Tawnja walking away from my door saying, "he must be in bed." I opened the door and invited all to come in. It was Dennis, Barb, Tawnja, Mike Moore, the new high school principal and Catherine somebody, who was doing an in-service at the school. Tawnja brought salmon and moose steaks and Barb brought wine, a rice dish, cookies, bananas and fruit for me, plus a cheesecake with cherries for topping. They stayed until 10. Dennis stayed over night and went hunting with me the next morning. We had lots of fun visiting.

Dennis and I walked the property hunting, but didn't see anything. When we got back to the cabin we were talking at about 10, when in came Chris Hladick and his son Ben. Chris was the city manager for Dillingham. It was great to see them. They have a cabin in Estes Park, Colo. They had just returned to Dillingham from there yesterday. We had a nice visit.

Dennis left for Dillingham at 11: 30, as Barb was bringing up a tire to replace the flat on his jeep. He has x-country practice this afternoon and said he would be back out tonight. (However, he didn't make it.)

I worked staining the cabin around the windows and the trim. I also put medal on the toilet roof. Hauled some stone from the beach for the walkway. When Dennis had not arrived by 6, I ate some leftover salmon and was just drinking some milk and one of Barb's cookies when Dennis, Barb and Bill Darling drove up. Barb brought stew, homemade bread, wine and blueberry cobbler. She also brought me some more fruit. What a peach! They stayed until 9:45 and Dennis returned with them as he had a meet in Anchorage over the weekend. Said he hoped to be back out Sunday night.

8-25-00 Got up at 7 and went east of the cabin with my boat and hunted the open parks on the north shore. Didn't see anything. Got back to the cabin about 10 and started hauling stone for the path. Picked some blueberries behind the cabin and after three loads of stones I decided to make some blueberry pancakes. I finished the first two when I heard a knock on the door. It was John Norman who had walked over from his lodge. He asked if he could use my boat to pull his large boat to the landing for repairs. Said he had an engine to use. I said that he could use my boat so he left with it.

Refrigerator stopped working. It was freezing everything, but now it doesn't work at all. Tried turning off the gas and running it on electric, but that didn't work either. I have a pan of left over stew, along with cheesecake and blueberry pancake batter, which I will use up shortly.

Went in the kayak at 3:30 and when I went past John's I thought I saw my boat there. His big boat was gone. I paddled until about 5:30 and as I approached the shore of a small bay I could see a lynx sitting on the shore, looking at me. I took out my video camera and started taking pictures of it as it walked along the lakeshore. He would walk a few steps then stop and look my way. In just a few minutes he disappeared into the brush and trees. Since he was walking on a peninsula toward the other bay, I decided to paddle around the peninsula and see if he would come out the other side. I turned the kayak around and quickly paddled around the point. I no more than got to the other side and he stepped out of the brush onto the shore. I started my camera again. The lynx would walk a few steps, then stop and look at me. I was not more than 20 feet from him. He was behind brush and tree limbs part of the time, but didn't hesitate to walk through openings. I followed him down the beach for about 50 yards and he then disappeared into the brush.

I decided to paddle away from the shore and head down the bay farther. Looking back every few minutes to see if he had reappeared on the beach, I was rewarded to see, not him, but a porky stroll onto the beach. He was very light colored and headed in the direction I was paddling. A few minutes later the lynx appeared behind the porky. I wondered if he was going to attack the porky, but he didn't. Instead, he disappeared into the trees and that was the last time I saw him. He was the first lynx I had ever seen in the wild. I headed back to the cabin with some video I would share with others.

I just finished a bath out of a pan, since I can't get the hot water heater to work, to take a shower. I washed out some underwear and socks, and started a fire in the wood stove. Feels good. It started raining about 5:30.

Rained the night and is still raining this morning. Looks like it will rain all day. I'll hunt by looking out the window. Lots of reading today. I want to call Gail today, as it was too late last night after John got back. He has to set up his satellite phone outside. Guess it does not take long, but I didn't want to ask him to do it in the rain.

Well, it is getting a little cool in here so I'll start the wood stove again. It is still raining out and is about 50. Glad I'm not in a tent. Reminds me of some other times we have been out in the tent with rain and high winds.

Here it is 2:00 p.m. and I just finished another book. This one was called the Seekers. I'm anxious to talk to Gail.

So far I have spent a total of $5.00 for a padlock for my gun case, $15.00 for gas and $15.00 for food.

I made an inventory of most of the things I have up here that are exclusively mine. I'm sure there are other things such as dishes, pots and pans, etc that I brought up to the cabin when I moved from Dillingham.

8-27-00 Got up at 7 and went down to the area where I got shot. Saw a grizzly bear along the beach and took some video of him. This is the same bay where several years ago I was motoring slowly down the bay and was watching three caribou walking along the beach. It appeared to be a cow with two yearlings. I heard another outboard running and turned around to see a boat approaching. In it was a gray haired native man. He motored up to me and asked if I was going after the caribou. I told him that I was not and if he wanted them to go after them. He said, "thanks" and motored toward them. The caribou were unconcerned and continued to walk and stop. He motored up within 50 yards and shot twice. He didn't hit anything and they ran a short distance up the beach, not into the woods and began walking. He started his engine and went closer. He again shut off his engine and shot twice more. This time he hit one and he went on to the beach to dress it out.

I didn't see anything else after going on down to the end of the bay, so I headed back to the cabin.

I put up a light fixture in the dinning area and got a bulb from John and it really brightens up the area.

Must have rained over two inches. That was about how much I found in the wheelbarrow. Partly cloudy this morning and about 50. Need to wash dishes. Just finished hauling stone from the beach to cover the path to the outhouse. Worked up a sweat. No bugs today. Breeze from the west.

The moose are not in the rut yet and don't seem to be moving much. Should come up later for moose. Caribou are not in the area yet either.

My radio has been my company. Lots of different kinds of music on NPR. Some of it was classical from festivals in Aspen and Vail. Some of the music made me feel sad.

Tried calling home, but there was no answer. I did get a hold of daughter, Tamlynn, using John's satellite phone. Nice to hear her voice and that of the girls. Sorry Gail was not home. Also tried son, Scott, but there was no answer. John and Nancy invited me over for dinner tonight. Their guests had plane connection problems so they will not be here until sometime tomorrow. They feel that's fine, as it gives them a little break. We had cheeseburgers, chips, wine, onions, and homemade chocolate ice cream. Jeff, Brent and Anna, employees, were there also. Brent and Anna are college students. Brent is from Wisconsin and Anna is from Anchorage. Jeff is a teacher on a one years leave of absence. All seem very nice. Jeff graduated from Western Michigan University.

Got up at 6:30 and went hunting in the kayak. Have to save on gas. Paddled the shoreline for three and one half-hours and only saw two beaver, which I videoed. When I got back to the cabin, even though it is overcast and looks like rain, I varnished my boat seat and the front of the steam.

Dennis has not shown up and I suspect he won't until later this evening, if at all. He left his stuff here, so I expect he will return sometime.

I'm thinking about leaving here before the 5th. Don't know if I can get my ticket changed or not, but I've done all the work that needs doing around here. It is lonely without someone else around and I guess I don't care if I shoot a moose or a caribou.

Started a fire in the wood stove and began reading another book, my third. That says a lot about what is going on around here. I should have brought 10-15 gal of gas instead of one tank and one 5 gal can. I did use about 5 gal of gas I had here in one of my tanks. I have been trying to conserve, so therefore I'm not out hunting or fishing.

Took a walk behind the cabin about 6:30 p.m. and didn't see anything. Warmed up Barb's stew, had some cheesecake and crackers. Wished Gail was here to share the quietness and warm fire. At about 7 it started raining and the wind blew hard. I am going to bed. Got back up at 8 because I couldn't sleep. Decided I would leave and see if I can get my ticket changed to leave ASAP. Packed up some things and carried them upstairs. Went back to bed around 9 and listened to the howling wind and rain. We got gusts up to 50 knots. Most of the time the wind blew between 20-40 knots. Doesn't look like I will be able to leave until it slows down. Instead of going outside about 3 to pee, I found a bucket to use. It was much more convenient.

At 12:30 p.m. the wind has died down, but it is still raining. I went out and bailed out the boat, which took about 20 minutes. I rolled up the hoses used to pull water out of the lake into the water tank upstairs and put them away; filled the generator with gas and added a can of stable. I didn't use it much, but it is now ready for winter. All I need to do now is shut off the propane and drain the water tank. I cleaned up the storage inside the house and the steam, also. It is 3:30 and still blowing and raining. Would like to try and call Gail again, but I don't want to ask John because he has to set up his satellite equipment outside on a bench. He is charged even if I use a credit card, so when I used it last I gave him $10.00 even though he didn't want to take it. My eyes are tired from reading. Am anxious to get back home.

6:30 p.m.—I have everything packed, including Dennis' gear. What—the sun just came out. However, the wind seems to have picked up again. I have decided I'm leaving in the morning come hell or high water. I can now see small patches of blue sky. Just finished my third book. Got the inventory of all my stuff done so I won't have to wonder what is here.

Got up at 7 and left for Dillingham at about 8. Got the boat on the trailer by 8:40 and was at Dean's by 9.

Barb was there and when I told her I was leaving she said, "You can't leave for at least a half hour."

I said, "why?"

She said, " You have a surprise coming."

I could not think of any kind of surprise I would have coming since she didn't know I was going to come this morning. We talked a few minutes and a vehicle drove in, the house door opened and who should walk in, but son Scott. I could not believe my eyes. What a great surprise! We hugged each other and he introduced me to his friend from Colorado, by the name of Dennis. He then said there was another surprise and we needed to get to the airport to pick him up – Mike Rosa. Mike had been on a number of prior hunts in Alaska.

Scott and Dennis came in last night and wanted to come up to the cabin then, but were talked out of it because it was too nasty out. They stayed with Barb and Dennis and then went over to help Dave put up two walls on his new garage, the next morning. Dennis had gone over to Dave's to pick them up and I arrived at Dennis's and Barb's unexpectedly. Scott had planned this surprise visit a week earlier and called Dave and Tawnja to work out the details. Barb and Dennis were also involved in the plan.

Barb baked several loaves of bread, for us to take to the cabin. After we went to town to get more gas, caribou licenses, food and drink, we headed to the lake, with Scott and Dennis driving one of Barb and Dennis' cars and Mike and I in Tawnja's vehicle. Scott and Dennis had also blown up my Achilles so we put it on top of the boat and hauled it up to the lake. It worked fine.

Got up about 8. It was raining, so we had a leisurely breakfast and then decided to go drive the peninsula east of the cabin where I saw the bear earlier. We left the cabin about 9:30. We would hunt first and then go over to Icy Creek and fish. By the time we were done hunting, which produced only a brief sighting of two moose by Scott and Mike, the drivers, we were somewhat wet and cold. We went over to the creek, but there were no fish at the mouth or up the stream, so we headed back to the cabin and built a fire. It is about 3 and all three of them are sleeping.

The next day we went up to Sunshine Valley to fish. Mike and I walked up one of the riverbanks, he to fish and me to hunt. Scott and Dennis were at the other river mouth fishing. When Mike and I returned, he went over to another little stream that emptied in the lake and I walked back to see Scott and Dennis. They had anchored the boat just off the mouth of the river and were fishing. In the water were 8 others, two of them women, who were catching fish after fish. Scott and Dennis were not catching anything. Shortly after I arrived they came in with their "tails" between their legs. The two women out fished them. We then went down to the mouth of the other river where Mike was cleaning some reds (9) he had caught. Scott hooked a nice fish, which jumped several times before breaking his line. After the two boats left with the 8 people we went back up to the other river where Scott caught a nice silver salmon. I got two dolly vardens and Dennis caught two smaller dolly's. We had the silver for dinner.

Dead Caribou Bags Hunter

Figure 68 Scott with his nice silver salmon.

Figure 69 Me with my salmon.

Figure 70 Mike with his salmon.

We went east to the bay where I got shot. We decided to climb over the mountain at the lowest end. Scott and Mike said there was a trail to follow. Well, we walked down the open parks to the lowest end and didn't find the trail, so Mike and I cut up into the woods and Dennis and Scott went together. We were to whistle if we found the trail. We didn't find it and came out on top of the lowest hill well before they did. They found the trail just before they came out. We were well up the next hill before we saw them behind us. Mike and I sat down at about 12:00 noon to look over the tundra northeast of Jackknife Mt. We saw a large bull moose out about a quarter of a mile away. His white antlers gave him away. I climbed up on another hill above Mike. Scott and Dennis finally arrived and I went down to see them. We lost track of the first moose, but saw another one a bit closer. Scott, Mike and I decided to walk out and see how big he was. I had the moose license, so I would decide if I would shoot it. When we got where we last saw the moose, it was not apparent. Mike stood at one end of the brushy and tall grass area and Scott and I started walking in another direction. Mike took several steps into the tall grass and the moose rose up in front of him. He looked at Mike while Mike counted four brow tines on one side and three on the other. His antlers spread a bit over 60 inches, by Mike's estimate.

Scott and I saw the moose running and I decided not to shoot it with my gun, but I videoed it instead, until he disappeared. We walked a bit further to a ridge and I saw a bull caribou running away from us and I yelled at Scott, pointing at the caribou. We both shot and one of us hit it in the hind leg. We followed it toward where Dennis was setting, but it headed to the west and then lay down. We motioned to Mike to come up and shoot it, but before he could get up to us the caribou got up and headed toward Dennis. We heard three shots, so we headed toward Dennis. When we got in sight of him he motioned to us where the bull had gone. We walked in that direction and saw the bull trying to get up. Mike shot him.

Right after Scott and I shot at the caribou I looked up by the top of the mountain and saw a grizzly eating berries. He then walked along the top of the mountain watching us. He was about 200 yards away. He disappeared over the top of the ridge as I videoed him.

Keith Evans

We dressed out the caribou and were on our way at about 5:30, after eating a lot of blueberries. We got to the boat about 7:30, after stopping many times for Dennis to rest. He was carrying too much weight on his front.

When we got back to the cabin about a half hour later, we hung the meat up in the shade and were shooting the bull, when Dennis stood up and started limping and hollering. Mike offered to shoot him and Scott offered him a drink of hard stuff. He didn't get either, as he was too busy trying to get the cramps out of his legs.

Figure 71 Me, Dennis and Mike at the meat pole by the cabin.

I asked son Scott why he changed his mind about coming to Alaska this fall. According to Scott, he started thinking after our last conversation that he may have his priorities screwed up. He finally decided he should be in Alaska hunting and fishing with his dad. Of course, his boss and co-workers got tired of him second guessing himself for not going to Alaska, and his boss told him to pack his bags and get to hell out of town. So he did, after talking Dennis, a construction friend, into coming along with him.

Dennis got a bit more exercise than his large body was used to, climbing up and down a mountain and packing out some meat. He experienced seeing bull moose, a grizzly bear, a wolf and getting three shots at a bull caribou. He also got the antlers of the caribou to

Dead Caribou Bags Hunter

take home. He earned them for helping haul the meat down the mountain; besides, Mike had all the caribou antlers he needed from prior successful hunts with us.

We spent the next several days fishing at the west end of the lake at a place called, "Sunshine Valley." We caught salmon and dolly varden. We also had some unexpected entertainment when Scott hooked a silver salmon and Dennis waded over to net it. Seems the salmon was smarter than Dennis, as he swan around a leg, which belonged to Dennis and avoided his swipes with the net. The salmon then departed and never stopped going. It wasn't the first one Scott lost off his fly rod, but it was the first one with that kind of entertainment.

We would again be leaving Alaska with fish, wild game and special memories.

Figure 72 Midnight sunset by cabin.

Keith Evans

ABOUT THE AUTHOR

Every since he was 12 years old, Keith Evans has been hunting and fishing.

In those early years the wild game and fish harvested by Keith and his brother, Red, were a needed supplement for the five children and mother in the family.

As a boy, Keith read stories by his favorite author, Jack London. Keith vowed that someday he would go to Alaska to hunt and fish.

After taking early retirement in Michigan., he accepted a school administrative position in Alaska, the fall of 1988.

In his book: *Dead Caribou Bags Hunter,* he shares his experiences from 1988 to 2000, which describe seventeen hunting and fishing adventures. He is lucky to be alive.

Printed in the United States
778400005B